LIFE, I SWEAR

LIFE, I SWEAR

INTIMATE STORIES FROM BLACK WOMEN ON IDENTITY, HEALING, AND SELF-TRUST

CURATED BY

Chloe Dulce Louvouezo

HARPER DESIGN

An Imprint of HarperCollins Publishers

LIFE, I SWEAR.

Copyright © 2021 by Chloe Dulce Louvouezo.

HarperCollins books may be purchased for educational, business, or sales promotional use. For information, please email the Special Markets Department at SPsales@harpercollins.com.

First published in 2021 by
Harper Design
An Imprint of HarperCollins*Publishers*
195 Broadway
New York, NY 10007
Tel: (212) 207-7000
Fax: (855) 746-6023
harperdesign@harpercollins.com
www.hc.com

Distributed throughout the world by
HarperCollins*Publishers*
195 Broadway
New York, NY 10007

ISBN 978-0-06-307223-7

Library of Congress Control Number: 2021033075

Book design by Dominique Jones

Printed in Canada

First Printing, 2021

To Myel, our mamush. It begins and ends with you.
You are the catalyst to my bloom and my grounds for renewal.
We are growing up together with hearts intertwined.
I feel more human because of and with you.
You are the reason I never want to be erased from this world.
My stories will always be yours too.

To my late grandmother Joyce, who would exhale deeply, fascinated by the stories
that live in strangers. You planted the seed and told me to write a book,
knowing that even at ten years old, my life was ripe for blank pages. So I did.

To the family I've never known and the family I've lost.
Despite the mystery of each other, you remain a home base, a beginning,
and a checkpoint that informs my essence even in my wandering.

And to the young Black girls and women in every corner of the world.
This collection was curated with you in mind.
Our spirit cannot be denied because it vibrates from our veins.
Nothing can take what runs through us, so long as we know that to be true.

CONTENTS

PART III
PEACE IT TOGETHER

Foreword

Elaine Welteroth

I met Chloe in 2012. When I say I met her, I don't mean we shook hands and made polite small talk. I mean from sunrise to sunset, we curled up like kittens at the foot of our mutual sister-friend's bed in Harlem as I listened intently to her tales of harrowing betrayals and crushing blows that she weathered with heroic grace. In a world where most wade into the shallow waters of new friendship slowly and with cautious optimism, we joined hands and cannonballed right into the deep end. And in those deepest of waters, I saw straight into her soul. Little did she know then, I'd journeyed a parallel path in love that led to a nearly identical heartbreak I hadn't yet processed and a rebirth I was still undergoing. When she cracked open her broken heart to let me in, I felt blood drip from my own . . .

If that sounds dramatic, it was.

That's because in all my twenty-something years on this planet, never had I met someone who I felt so instantly connected to, someone whose mere existence held up a mirror to my own polarities. It would be cliché to call her a kindred spirit, but I couldn't shake this knowing that our lives were divinely intertwined.

We'd joke that we were made from the same stardust. So it never came as a surprise when we attracted the exact same men or when we even got mistaken for twins by strangers. It just felt like physical evidence of what we both knew to be true in the spirit realm—in each other, we had found an extension of ourselves. But it was much more than just the physical resemblance that struck me. The resemblance was soul-deep. A healer seeking the path toward healing. A free-spirited adventurer and a pragmatic perfectionist warring over which will take the wheel at any given moment. The trusting naivete of a kid at heart with the stubborn resilience of a woman warrior who may have shed blood in the battle but refuses to lose the war. In each of her contradictions, I saw my own.

Since the start of our sisterhood that fateful Super Soul Sunday in Harlem, we've lived lifetimes together and co-created many more harrowing tales. Along the way, I've had the privilege of witnessing Chloe's resilience on repeat in real time as her life has continued to unfold with one remarkable act of faith after another. As a sister, I feel the pain and joy in her experiences as if they were my own. As a fellow writer and author, I am jolted by the impact of the poetic honesty in her words.

Now, as she prepares to bravely share many of those stories with and for you—stories that bonded us back then—I am overwhelmed with a sense of pride to write alongside her and so many other Black women warriors whose narratives fit into a larger tapestry of our collective traumas and triumphs.

This book is an embodiment of the power of all the untold stories that bond us. Each one an essential part of our collective experience as Black women.

Across the diaspora, Black women are so often the backbones of our families. The prayer warriors. The protectors. The strong friends. The ride or die's. The teachers and healers of the world. A world that has turned its back on us throughout history. Still, we rise, but who can we count on to hold us down? We do so much explaining of ourselves, of our value, of our identities, yet so much of who we are is never truly seen or understood. The exception to that rule is when we are in the presence of our sisters. There is an immediate exhale, an intimacy even in the wordless exchanges that reset our nervous systems and fill our bodies with a sense of safety.

That's because our stories are as intertwined as our traumas. The same is true of our healing. Each time I let someone hold a piece of my heart that's been hurt before. When a sister-friend trusts me with her truth. When an elder tells her story for the first time. When we listen—really listen and hold sacred space for sisterhood, we instantly come into awareness that we are all more interconnected than we realize.

What I know for sure is this: There is so much healing locked up in the stories Black women never tell. But a powerful ripple effect is set into motion with each tidal wave of truth that is introduced to the collective consciousness. This is how radical healing happens.

The inverse is also true. When we withhold or hide the parts of ourselves that need healing, we rob the collective of becoming whole.

Because here's the thing about healing: It isn't linear and it's never just about you. When we heal our wounds, that healing is felt across lifetimes and lineages. Generational chains are broken when we engage each other in the process of the inner work we simply cannot do alone.

When you tell your truth, I become more accountable to my own. When I engage in the brave act of acknowledging my pain aloud, it gives you permission to access yours, too. We become mirrors to and for each other.

Your healing is my healing.
Your freedom is my freedom.
Your work is my work.
Your peace is my peace.

How would you show up differently in the world if you knew this were true?
How much more honest would you be?
How much more grace would you give?
How would you show up differently as a friend, sister, daughter, and mother?

Each story in this book extends an invitation to you to dive deeper into your own self-reflective journey in order to access deeper levels of healing that can only happen in sacred community. This book offers a safe space for Black women to feel seen in our most vulnerable and authentic truths. Through Chloe's meticulous curation, she invites you into a community that blossoms with each breakthrough and that challenges you to do the work you were put here to do.

The Space We Deserve

Chloe Dulce Louvouezo

This book is an undertaking of the heart. Life, I swear. To me that saying captures it all. The irony, the challenge, the faith, the resilience, the sweet manifestation, the ugly chaos, and the calm—all the ebbs and flows that frame how we experience and interpret this life.

"Life, I swear" was one of those things my girlfriends and I would exhale after long conversations about how the growing pains both depleted and revived us. "Life, I swear" became how we described polarities that brought irony to our feelings and to the realities of our worlds. It is these polarities and the stories that form them that make us human.

In my midtwenties, I took a one-way bus to New York City with one bag, no job, and the curiosity to find out what life could offer if I finally gave back what I had deprived myself of until then: forgiveness of the imperfections of my journey. I committed to extending myself an olive branch—to make peace with the ways in which I had been hard on myself. My sister-friends Brooke, Elaine, and Offeibea became my handpicked family, filling the voids where blood and lustful love lacked or disappointed. In confidence and in trust, we validated each other as we fumbled our way through figuring life out and gave ourselves permission to live in both faith and fear. In those coming-of-age years, we were forced to face some hard truths about our regrets and immaturities. God was requiring us to lean into clumsy and uncomfortable seasons of maturing, while also teaching us what forgiveness and being kind to ourselves meant. It was through this sisterhood that we experienced emotional alchemy—a journey of mindfulness of our vulnerabilities, our faith, and our innate wisdom. And it was through our shared intimacy that we grew deeper intimacy with ourselves that rooted us in the beauty of our stories.

I love stories. I love the texture and the nuances of them. I love understanding our *why*s of everything. Why do we feel the way we feel, and what makes us do the things we do? For Black women, being in community as we unpack and make sense of our whys and our lives is an outlet that nothing else in the world can provide. Our sharing of uncertainties, vulnerabilities, and trepidations about life makes space for a special intimacy—an intimacy we are rarely afforded because the

world expects the strength of Black women to be demonstrated through restraint of our true selves. Challenging seasons of life remind us how much intimacy and feeling understood are gateways to personal healing. After a trying year in 2019, I started to document conversations with other Black women about personal stories that have enlightened us to answer some of these questions: as deep-dive dialogues in my *Life, I Swear* podcast and as stories in this book.

I've always considered myself a cat with nine lives, rebirthed in each new season—one that emerges from fires at times scarred but layered in stories that together tell the tale of the dance of this life. It's been an incredible one. I've lived in eleven cities, five countries, and traveled the world. I've been in abusive and loving relationships, home birthed a prince of a son, grew a family, been a single mother raised by a single mother. I've taken risks, led a spontaneous life, explored artistry, and ebbed and flowed through loss and glory. Tell me something you've been through and I bet I can relate. Give me a story of promise and hope and faith, and you're speaking to my spirit. Give me a story of pain and struggle, and know in my eyes that I deeply understand.

I spent years trying to find the words to articulate the breadth of what this journey of life has meant to me. Putting pen to paper through stories of love and loss, discovery and rebounds is the only way I know how. The pages that follow are an anthology of stories from Black women about the falling down, the cycles, the post-traumatic growth, and the resilience. In curating these stories, I've had the blessed opportunity to speak to other women of the Black diaspora from around the country and the world, all who have shared from a place of vulnerability and truth. Their stories capture a range of experiences and reflections that offer nuance and variation of our human nature to discover new facets of ourselves. They represent voices and sentiments of our time, chronicled for our collective healing.

Being honest in my own storytelling and being receptive of others' has helped me find the grace in "still figuring it all out." I offer this collection of stories today knowing what I didn't know in earlier life seasons: that the most interesting stories are not ones of shame or regret. The most interesting stories are ones of

self-examination, where we examine our own involvement in decisions and our complicated emotions that, in examining them, lead us to grow. With all we are reckoning with in the country and in our own heads around the value of Black lives and voices, we have to come back to our own sense of value to free ourselves and to feel a sense of grace.

It took me a while to get to a place of grace and acceptance that comes from self-examination. I was wary of what might become of my sense of self if I looked too closely at some hard truths about my traumas and immaturities. Finding our bearings and being vulnerable enough to examine and share our wounds before they are healed is an act of courage that I wasn't prepared for. Sharing prematurely bears the risk of retriggering ourselves. So for years I kept my stories to myself, swept away in the dusty corners of my memory, waiting until the day that I felt fully resolved with them to be *qualified* to share. I've learned though, through less compartmentalizing and more flow, that you can in fact be a mess and a messenger at the same time. You can, in fact, need healing while also helping others heal. You can be proud of your growth while also needing to be inspired, redirected, or humbled. You can struggle with the ambiguity of the future but still honor the essence of who you are, which is often the only thing we know for sure. And you can wonder in disillusionment of God's plan—*why me, why this*—while still being supremely grateful for Her omnipresence. The expectation of strength being antonymous to still working through our fragilities can pressure us to bottle in how we are processing life and and can lead to self-doubt siloed, and makes intimacy through vulnerability nearly impossible.

We have to give ourselves permission to allow the polarities of our present moment or our identities to exist in the same space. For a long time, I struggled to recognize this and refrained from divulging myself to others. As a nomad who moved from city to

> **Finding our bearings and being vulnerable enough to examine and share our wounds before they are healed is an act of courage that I wasn't prepared for.**

WE NEED
EACH OTHER
RIGHT NOW
AND ALWAYS.

city all my life, I know what uncertainty feels like and for years wrestled with not having a sense of belonging. Relationships always felt fleeting, trust was sparse, and permanence was rare. To share parts of myself with others felt like a sacrifice, to relinquish the guarantee of reciprocal vulnerability. But when I began to share my untold stories with people I love and the community I was building, kindred connections and personal healing followed. Recounting experiences that had once felt life- and soul-threatening was a love offering to my people and to myself. It contextualized the pieces they knew of me and welcomed them to explore the pieces of life we had yet to uncover together. And finally, I could be me, stripped and naked in my truth. When we tell our stories enough times in safe spaces, we release the burden or weight they carry. There is nothing left to conceal, not from others, not from myself. This is me, ugly and beautiful, brave and sometimes still terrified. But whole, alive, and well.

Had it not been for the women in my life who listened, who ushered me into each rebirth in the changing seasons, and who helped me honor my own resilience, I wouldn't have had the courage to share my polarities out loud. Sisterhood, as both universal and intimate as it is, reminds us that we do not have to journey alone. It makes room for us to just be and invites all of our stories, humanly flawed, to exist as the sum of who we are. In doing so, I've learned to leverage my sense of self and identity to support others in being at peace with their own through introspective celebration.

Black women especially deserve this space. I hope the stories that follow encourage you to honor the nuances of your own and to make more space for all the ways Black women process our lives. The journey of making this book come together has been insanely therapeutic. I hope you turn the pages feeling encouraged to be present in your journey and to give yourself permission to love on yourself a little more, and always a little more. I hope you find solace in seeing yourself through the stories of other women. We need each other right now and always.

With love,
Chloe Dulce Louvouezo

Coming Home to Ourselves

Chloe Dulce Louvouezo

How do you greet yourself at the door when you knock, having been away for a while? If you left yourself long enough to no longer recognize the scars on your own hands and the tear traces on your own cheeks, battered or numb, how do you welcome yourself back in? You make space for her to sit. You fix her a cup of tea and you rest in silence together, leaving air for her to recount all that she's been through while away, disengaged from her center, which is you.

She describes the stories behind each scar and each trace down her face. They were not in vain. They were collected through the fires she endured and those she extinguished, and she came home to you, to herself, to impart the revelations they revealed. Sometimes she needs consoling, a tender landing place as respite from the world. Sometimes she needs a revival as assurance that she can withstand life outside your door if she leaves you again.

You meet her where she is with the foresight to know any words you share will pierce her deeply. She is fragile about her personal narrative. You've been here before with her, with yourself, enough times to know that what she really needs is conviction of confidence to stand tall again. In every way, the world told her to bend down and collapse. And beyond her stoicism you know her delicacy and that she almost did. Her stories returned her bruised; it is your job to remind her of their impermanence, as her person, her one and only. Sit and bask in the pride of survival together. Hold hands and know the light you carry behind your shadow is your nobility. Your stories brought you home to yourself with dignity, and your light is always on. Welcome home.

YES, SIS.

This book is for women who know women,
and for women who love women.

For women whose identities have been
questioned or whose heartaches have cut
through their sense of self over time.

This is for Black women whose voices have
been silenced to the point of disassociation.

And for those who kept their stories to
themselves, waiting on pride or fear to pass.

It's also for women who believe that healing is
our birthright and that joy cannot be stolen.

For women who trust the liberation and
learning that come from sharing and listening.

Our stories are ours, and they are sacred.

This book is for us.

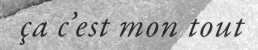

ça c'est mon tout

PART I

SUM OF
MY PARTS

Our Stories Affirm Us

Our stories are full of nuances, character, and dualities. As I've grown to understand the richness and texture of my own life, I find liberty in not boiling my existence as a Black woman down to a single identity, a linear path, or a limited awareness of myself. None of us are from just one place or experience. We are the sum of our parts—we are every moment, memory, and ancestor that has beautifully crafted who we are today. Ask me who I am and I will go down a list of sights, sounds, energies, and lineages that define me. When we embrace our dimensions, we can sink more deeply into ourselves and tell our stories with more reverence.

Hues of Exposure

Chloe Dulce Louvouezo

For so long, being asked where I was from would make me physically cringe. I've never lived in any city long enough for it to be my own. I've stuttered on this question because I'm from many places and nowhere at the same time. Not having an answer to offer felt like a barrier to others getting to know me, so I adjusted my reply based on what I assumed they would understand. At least, I'd think to myself, they could relate to that part of my story. But it felt inauthentic to represent myself as being "from" anywhere, because not one part of my story could ever illustrate me in full. For so long I was a passerby, never having spent more than three years in any one city. While I've had the blessing of having a window into many communities and cultures, I haven't been rooted to any place in particular.

Home has been a very temporary notion my entire life. Now in my midthirties, I've lived in five countries, eleven cities, twenty-five homes, and with eight families. By all definitions, I'm a Third Culture Kid: I spent my childhood immersed in cultures different from my Congolese and American parents' before I fully developed my own identity. Even before adulthood I was a nomad. My mother worked in international development, and as a single mother, she followed opportunity. By age seven, I had lived in Brazzaville, Congo; Los Angeles;

Washington, DC; and Princeton, New Jersey. After second grade, her work relocated us across the world to Niamey, Niger, a place that would forever change my life.

Niger was where I felt most at ease. There is so much nostalgia attached to my memories of Niger. It was the smell of the burning wood at night that carried across the neighborhoods with the dry light breeze, and the scent of the sun-exposed fruits at the market as men rushed by with bootleg CDs of Brandy and Monica. It was the sun-filled streets and the sandy dirt roads outside our houses, young boys selling bubble gum and cigarettes at the street corners by day, and men crowded around box television sets on those same street corners at night, cheering loudly at the soccer games flickering on the screens as they held the antennas still. Girls dipping my fingertips and the palms of my feet into burnt orange henna between giggles, and women tugging at my scalp as they wrapped each strand into braids while I sat between their warm thighs. It was the daily calls from the mosque that echoed through the city, slowing the traffic and the pace of the day. My life in Niger gave me a sense of place—an understanding that the conditions around us give texture to our experiences. Yet, neither the city nor the culture were mine.

Within the walls of our international expatriate community was a true melting pot. I had friends and teachers from around the world, from Japan to Mexico, Lebanon to Germany, and like me, many of my friends didn't look like their parents—adopted, mixed, and of all shades. Between home, school, and the bustle of the city, it was typical to hear ten languages and be exposed to ten cultures in one day, and they all left their footprint on me. Some days, I'd spend afternoons at my Nigerian friend Tunrayo's house watching reruns of Nollywood flicks, and other days were spent in the kitchen of my Gambian friend Aminata's house watching her mother cook yassa fish and peanut stew dinners while she read lines from the Koran with her Arabic tutor. The diversity of the intercontinental African diaspora was as rich as it was common among the Ivorian, Kenyan, Tunisian, and Burkinabe friends that surrounded me. I only had faint memories of Congo at that point, but because my white mother's affinity to Africa was stronger than it was to America, my being African was never in question.

While I was often mistaken for a native of Niger—Nigerien—on my own, walking alongside my mother with her freckled skin and green eyes revealed that it wasn't my native land—it othered me. I was the daughter of an *anasara*—a white person—and by default also considered one myself by many Nigeriens, which was less about race than it was about privilege. The teas-ing children who'd tag behind us at the flea market and the elderly women who held their hands out for change at the stoplights would echo "anasara, anasara, anasara" in a chant. I remember walking through a rural market in Baleyara one scorching-hot afternoon with my mother, a regular day trip to collect beads, baskets, and woven blankets for her craftwork that adorned our home in Niamey. We pushed through the thick crowd of vendors and merchants, and I tried to keep up with my mother's pace as we tailed behind another mother and daughter in front of us. When the child turned around, she burst into horrified tears at the sight of my mother. The child's mother explained that the girl had never seen an anasara before in her life and was naturally shaken by her first sighting. As we continued through the market, my eyes caught gazes from vendors and shoppers in my direction. Those gazes—intentional or curious—questioned my affinity to my mother as much as to them, who were of my same complexion. That was the start of a yearslong struggle to find balance in being uncomfortably pulled between African and American, kinship and foreigner, Black and white, and privilege and poverty. My experience in Niger sat at an intersection of all of those things.

The difference between life within the insularity of the expatriate world and the realities

Because my white
mother's affinity to
Africa was stronger
than it was to
America, my being
African was never
in question.

that lived outside those walls was polarizing. The economic poverty and prolonged droughts distressed the conditions of the country. You could see it in the barren landscape, the scarcity of jobs, and the restlessness of the youth. Bearing witness to chronic poverty at such a young age did something to me. It awakened an early awareness of differences in privilege and access—things defined by inequitable opportunity for economic mobility that draw lines between countries, communities, and cultures. While I lived as an American expatriate, my years there were an onboarding of learning how to navigate a spectrum of social conditions and identities. Niger's reserved culture and Islamic influences in the 1990s modeled a humility I've never known elsewhere, and I learned quickly that etiquette and perspective accompany context. Around the city, I knew to carry myself mindfully and consciously in my transition from one world to another. The window I had into both Niger's humility and Islam and into the rest of Nigerien culture showed me early on how to be thoughtful about how I navigate others' perceptions of me.

My mother first moved to Niger in her early twenties, and this sparked a love affair with the country that kept returning her to Niamey and the neighboring villages and towns throughout her life. Her settling down in West Africa was her rebellion against the homogeneity of the white America she knew from the 1960s. It was also an opportunity for her to single-parent with more ease than the escalating bills and cramped studio apartments would allow in the United States. Niger was an unlikely but fitting refuge for her because it spoke to her sensibilities, and she groomed me to appreciate the significance of all it had to teach me. Like her, I grew an intimate relationship with Niger, and like her, I learned to navigate a world so different from my own by not just having a relationship with the people but also with the place itself.

But by high school, the affinity I had with Niamey was replaced by wanting to withdraw. I mistook familiarity for boredom. I retreated to the library at the American Cultural Center to discover new places. Over an afternoon of reading through books on American boarding schools, I chose one that felt good and then made a case to my mother. The demands of her career

Constant assimilation to so many contexts impeded me from getting to know myself outside of their labels.

had taken precedence over her capacity to be hands-on. The self-agency she raised me with was something of which I think we were both proud, though it gave me more autonomy than a typical teenager, which at the time I took for granted. That fall I packed my bags. When my mother dropped me off at boarding school in Tacoma, Washington, I remember her walking out of the dorm building and into the Pacific Northwest rain. I immediately mourned the impermanence of my years under the Saharan sun.

Outside of Niger, no other place has felt inviting enough to sink into. I have called the quaint tree-lined sidewalks of Striver's Row in Harlem home; the cactus-lined backyards of Tucson, Arizona; the bustling markets of Bamako, Mali; and the rolling hills of Kigali, Rwanda. When I was younger, my mother's career wasn't conducive to raising a child conventionally. The nature of it took her to remote towns in the desert terrains of Niger. Meanwhile, I lived with a Liberian family and a Canadian family; and when I came to the United States, I lived with a Black American family and on a reservation with a Sioux Native American family. These were family friends or families of my friends. Some my mother knew, some she didn't know at all. The trust she had in me and of people forged my independence in choosing the spaces I entered and the relationships I cul-

tivated. Living with other families who offered their homes to me and abiding by their ways—their food, their language, their philosophies—expanded my worldview and consciousness of difference with each relocation. I felt less like a guest in their homes than sometimes within my own family's I cut my teeth on race in America at a predominantly white boarding school, then a predominantly Black public school, and found solace with my Blackness in America on the hilltop of Howard University, a place that had felt so mystical, that I needed to uncover. These are all places rich in memories that have together made up the sum of my parts, each distinctly offering a new discovery of both culture and of the untapped parts of me their environments revealed. The muscle it took to constantly acclimate when I was younger made me agile and adaptable, which I didn't learn to leverage until years later in adulthood.

I have evolved into a fusion of all these places and communities. But being too adaptable without the anchor of a rooted culture

or home of my own was also the handicap of nomadic life. It wasn't until my repatriation to the States as a teenager that I understood how my cultural "homelessness" set me up to acclimate to an unfamiliar and confusing racial context in America. The distinction between being Black and being African was made clear, as were some people's distinctions between being Black and being mixed. And the comparison of being mixed American in sub-Saharan Africa to how I experienced race in America crystallized just how much Blackness is contextualized differently across the world. Constant assimilation to so many contexts impeded me from getting to know myself outside of their labels.

I rarely encountered others with journeys similar to mine. But Howard University welcomed intersectionality in a way that made anomalous experiences less alien. There wasn't the burden of having to explain myself or my identity. I didn't have to align with a linear experience as I did in other spaces, because The Mecca was a constellation of stories from across the global Black diaspora. The distinction of our journeys didn't matter as much as understanding that the world outside The Mecca would not celebrate Blackness as it was celebrated on the yard. It was in that common understanding that my reference for being Black in America took root.

The best part of my journey has been the process of translating duality into perspective. While the question of where I'm from can feel forced, the question of where home is allows us to think of home as more than a singular location and doesn't lock us into singular identities. I journey back home to myself because I now understand the nuances of how and why each place has labeled me differently, making its mark on who I am. There's a mutual exchange I believe we should all have with the communities we occupy. They give us nostalgic memories and build our character. In exchange, we treat the communities we live in as relationship partners to whom we show gratitude for everything they've poured into us. In the scope of a lifetime, we may have only been tourists to the places we've called home and that have held pieces of us, but they remind us of who we are and how we got here.

Some of Me

Eniafebiafe Isis Adewale
Writer and Poet

There's this quote, "And you, you scare people because you are whole all by yourself." Every time I read or see these words, I think of my mother. That's who and how I have understood her to be. She's the most intelligent woman I know. She's studied multiple religions, is an avid reader, and at seventy years old still has a thirst for knowledge and is both curious and fascinated by life. My mother has a quiet force about her and is extremely rooted and secure in herself. Her worth and value are never in question. She does not ask permission to be who she is. She does not require that she be understood. She has always told my sister and me that we are everything—no question, no argument. This unwavering knowledge is what I greatly admire about her, because most times, I'm not so sure.

Growing up in a small town—Lake Elsinore, California—where race was such an identifying factor wasn't easy. To have my identity hang on the color of my skin felt like a burden, because in America, race is a weight we carry. As a child I toggled between the words of affirmation that I received at home and the prejudice and bigotry I received outside of it. While Black Power as a statement and expression of pride felt powerful and unifying, being boxed in to a singular identity made me feel uncomfortable. Race does not make room for variation, does not immediately allow for

nuances. Race does not tell you who I am. It assumes that my Blackness is the sum of me instead of "some" of me, and for me to be seen and to be heard is to be understood infinitely. Not either/or but and/also.

Race does not tell you who I am. It assumes that my Blackness is the sum of me instead of "some" of me.

As a writer and the older I get, the more conscious I am both of how I use words and what words I use. Through story and conversation, listening, reading, and learning about others and their experiences, I am awakened to pieces and parts of myself that I'm unable to articulate and put language to. The willingness to lend myself to tender conversations about identity has been powerful. It is where much of my healing and the inner awakening has begun.

In my adolescence while trying to affirm my identity for myself, it was outside negative words and voices that dug holes into me, and I never rid myself of them. As a result, in adulthood, I've continued to fall into the cycle of negative self-talk, and this has become a stumbling

block in my phases of growth and healing. This inner voice of critique has continued to breed itself over the years, and I find that I vehemently fight it. It has become ritual to stand in front of the mirror or catch myself in moments of doubt and contradict. I remind myself, *You are who you say you are*.

I understand the concept of "becoming," as a journey, but I am in a phase of coming undone, examination, and rediscovery. I have strayed and continue to wander and wonder on my way. I've found it necessary to balance the desire of wanting my becoming to end with an arrival that is solid, stationary, and concrete with the reality that it is more malleable than this. If we are taught that our becoming must be like the traditional story with a beginning, arc, and singular ending, becoming can feel limiting. We want our stories to end with a final understanding, but sometimes there is no clear-cut ending. Instead, it might be "to be continued" or "and so…" or "but yet and still." Because even in our becoming, and in our arrival, we are still learning.

BECAUSE
EVEN IN OUR
BECOMING,
AND IN OUR
ARRIVAL,
WE ARE STILL
LEARNING.

The Sacred Return
ON ANSWERING THE ANCESTORS' CALL

Lauren Ash
Founder, Black Girl in Om

Returning home to Minneapolis was not in my plans. Being from the Midwest, I found living in Los Angeles was heaven. But in February 2020, I attended a church service in LA at Agape Spiritual Center, where I heard Reverend Michael Bernard Beckwith speak about the power of listening to the spirit. It moved me so much and triggered something that had been tugging on my heart.

For months, I had been receiving a series of spiritual dreams of ancestral messages encouraging me and whispering for me to return back home to Minneapolis. At first, I interpreted them metaphorically, but when I continued to have them, I realized those messages were literal and that I should listen to them.

My intention to return was to heal my family lineage and patterns of dysfunction that no

I knew that the more I deepened into my own healing practices, the more I would be able to show up in the way that I show up best, which is by holding space for my people in the midst of trauma.

longer served me. For years in my twenties, I had—consciously and unconsciously—pushed family away. But then I started to recognize emotional trauma that I experienced when I was younger. On my thirty-second birthday, for the first time in my life I named *family* as a value. I recognize that I can love and accept my family and what happened, because we're reflections of each other. We do the best we can with the tools that we are given. We show up as the versions of ourselves that sometimes still have more healing to do. As humans, until we do the healing work, we only replicate the same dysfunction within our original family structure with our relationships and partnerships. I was led back home by my Creator as a divine blessing and opportunity to reclaim the parts of myself that I didn't even know about. It has been the most challenging season of my entire life, but I believe that the biggest challenges bring the biggest blessings if only we rise to the moment.

I returned home to Minneapolis in March 2020, at the start of the COVID-19 pandemic and right before the death of George Floyd and the uprising that followed. I felt confused and wondered what my place was in it all. I had clearly been led back to be there, in close physical proximity to that very moment of catalyzing energy. It was traumatizing to be living in my city during such a heightened time of riots and curfews. I got plugged in through a group of community healers and activists in the Twin Cities. We all have a role to play, and everyone's role looks very different. The group was showing up in various ways, from delivering food to providing herbs to support those with respiratory conditions. I was showing up by turning inward. I knew that the more I deepened into my own healing practices, the more I would be able to show up in the way that I show up best, which is by holding space for my people in the midst of trauma. But I jumped into the role of supporting others without recognizing how in need of and deserving of support I also was. A friend reached out and asked if I needed help. I suggested she host a meditation for people who had been impacted, as if I wasn't. I joined the meditation call and found myself crying because I realized it was for me, too. I needed to hold space for myself just as I did for others.

Being back home with family is both grounding and not. It has helped me remember and discover my roots, but it's also very destabilizing because there are still so many core wounds that I'm picking at and working through. I've been learning so much about family, and I'm incredibly blessed because we have a lot of physical materials from my ancestors. Much of our family history has been archived in photographs and letters, both within our family and also within museums throughout the Midwest. The stories I've discovered about my ancestors have been quite profound and allowed me to connect with them more deeply and hone my spiritual practices. The idea of grounding myself within my family inherently grounds me within myself.

I pray and honor my ancestors, and sometimes things come to me through those practices. There's so much available to us if we only allow ourselves to be spiritually open to receive. I recognize that not every person, especially Black folk, has the photographs and letters like my family does. But we have traditions and rituals that were passed through generations in our collective families. There are complexities to our stories and our histories, and sharing them is our spiritual gift. It's not everyone's journey to

be the family historian, but the more we allow ourselves to get curious and receive and learn, it only benefits our journeys. Ancestral communication and learning about who my ancestors were and are has allowed me to reclaim so much of myself.

In a letter I read written to my ancestor, W. A. Warmsley, an influential railroad contractor at the turn of the century, someone described how much of a workhorse he was and how he overextended himself. It spoke so much to me because I discovered that he was also very sick. Learning that he was praised for his success, while also navigating health issues caused by overworking, stressed to me the importance of how I personally embody and practice rest and share a message of self-care with my community. It has helped me stand firmer in my purpose.

There are complexities to our stories and our histories, and sharing them is our spiritual gift.

Our ancestors' lives leave bread crumbs for us. Sometimes it's less about the accuracy of their stories than it is about honoring their memories, even if those memories are flawed. I'm less interested in what happened in family history than in how ancestors related to one another, because those are powerful stories to learn from. I believe that we always receive the information, insights, and wisdom if we only ask. There may be gaps and mysteries, but that's okay, because every question we ask opens us up to receive intuitively, spiritually, and energetically. Our ancestors' bread crumbs offer information about what patterns we're meant to heal. And just as we inherit trauma, I believe we also inherit healing.

The Loveward Journey

Gabrielle Williams

Sound and Energy Healer and Educator

When I was younger, I was missing a real understanding of who I was and my purpose in the world, and I searched for it in a lot of the wrong places. I associated my self-worth with external definitions of success in my accomplishments and career. Prestige was important. I wanted to be seen and have some approximation to my idea of power, which was coupled with a very unexamined life in which I wasn't aware of how to become the most fully realized version of myself. I had an itch to travel and discover the world so much that it was as if my spirit and my subconscious knew what I needed at the time. I had traveled a good deal before and had lived in Spain for a few years, and every time I went overseas, I had a taste of living a life that was all my own. The States didn't feel like enough. I was doing well in some areas, but I wasn't fitting into the world of politics that drove the city and the career path I was on. I wasn't great at my jobs and wasn't truly connecting with people. I felt a strong pull to leave and create a new story for myself.

I had been fascinated with Brazil for a while. I'd visited before, and every time I went, I felt something stir within me and I felt very alive there. Moving within the country's beauty and being immersed in Afro-Brazilian culture felt like home. Our shared ancestry pulsed through every cell in my body. I felt like this is how I should dance; this is how it should be. This is how I should communicate; this is my rhythm. I always tell people that Bahia is like a portal to a deep spiritual connection. I had cracked open the portal on other visits, but during one particular trip, it became clear that I was ready to completely dive in and see what was on the other side. During this visit, I had a cleansing and a reading done by a Mae de Santo, a priestess in the Afro-Brazilian religion Candomblé. I felt things during that session with her that I had never felt before—a tingling sensation followed by a release, like something inside me was melting. Tears were flowing, and a wave of gratitude and wonder washed over me. I knew I was just starting to scratch the surface of the mystery of spirit that Brazil held. She said I would return to live there, and her words stuck with me. I was dating a Brazilian American man back in DC at the time, and when he got a job in Salvador, Bahia, I jumped at the chance to move down with him. It's the cultural capital of Brazil and the largest African diaspora in the world, so I knew there was something there for me, and that something turned out to be a complete spiritual overhaul.

While in Bahia, I was able to build a new family. In hindsight, I know I was guided to them by my ancestors. I met a group of Black

American women who were immersed in various interlocking multilayered spiritual, artistic, and intellectual communities in Bahia. Within the community of Black Americans, we were all there to seek more connection with our African roots in ways we hadn't been able to fully do in the States, and that collective seeking is what brought us together. Those women introduced me to a whole new world by inviting me to a self-love, self-marriage ceremony at a beautiful quaint fishing village. It was in a tree house overlooking the most amazing beach I had ever seen. It was like a dream. We did a family constellation, which is a therapeutic technique where hidden family dynamics and damaging intergenerational patterns are discovered. A group of around seven unrelated people do a sort of workshop where they assist one member of the group who is facing difficulties, called the "seeker." A facilitator or therapist guides the seven to act as stand-ins for the seeker's family members. We basically started channeling these family members and illuminated the disharmony present in this particular person's family. I was chosen to represent a key family member, and as we were guided through the exercise, I began to feel the energy of that person vibrate within me and speak through me. I'd never connected with spirit in such an intense way, but this time I felt the same stirring in me that I had

felt during the cleansing ceremony by my Mae de Santo years before. Those women then introduced me to a wider community of Brazilian healers, shamans, and practitioners of all these amazing arts. That was really when everything completely changed for me.

On the night of my twenty-ninth birthday, we took a long journey to a shamanic community in the Atlantic Forest. We took part in a nightlong ayahuasca ceremony. It began as a frightening and confusing ride, but that gave way to intense visions that led to earth-shattering epiphanies. In one instance I was able to see through the eyes of my father, who had never been present in my life; I saw what he had experienced in Vietnam and watched his heart literally contract inside his chest. At that point I began to purge violently. But it wasn't nearly as terrible as it sounds—it was like letting go of the years of bitterness that his abandonment had calcified within me. I had never felt such a sense of relief in my life, and by morning I had experienced a 180-degree transformation—an awakening that brought me in tune with myself, the universe, and my purpose. Everything. I knew that this incredible medicine would be part of my life forever, but it wasn't until a few years later after working closely and frequently with my shamans that I would be asked to help others called to this healing path.

WHO I TRULY AM IS
LOVE AND LIGHT AND
PEACE AND UNIVERSAL
ENERGY. SOME DAYS I
CRY, WAIL, AND MOAN
ABOUT THE WEIGHT OF
LIFE, BUT THIS IS THE
JOURNEY. THE LIGHT
AND THE SHADOW.

Throughout my years in Bahia, I also started to shed layers of my Americanness. From my urgency, running about, always having to be entertained, or wanting things to go a certain way, I had to let that mess go in Bahia and be in spirit and move with the rhythm of life. But I was also very aware of the racial dynamics that played out in my experience. As a Black American woman, I straddled the different worlds of the city. I was connected with my Black intellectual artist friends and friends living in the favelas. But my American privilege was considered exotic and chic, and my English and professional life in teaching also gave me the opportunity to build friendships with upper-class, white Brazilians who lived in the wealthiest areas of the city. Despite being Black in a country that places value on colorism, my Americanness is what gave me access to a white world. In that way, I didn't experience racism in the same way I had experienced it in the States.

The most unexpected part of my journey in Brazil was finding out that I was pregnant on my thirtieth birthday. The combination of the threat of a miscarriage, a crumbling relationship, and the Zika pandemic incidentally brought me back to the States abruptly. The precariousness of my situation, including not having access to the best health care, had left me with few options. It was time to go home. I had been gone for five years, and gentrification had changed DC so much that I felt like I was on a new planet. It was the dead of winter. I was going through a breakup with my son's father. I couldn't find a job with my pregnant belly, so I didn't work for the first year. Add to that the fact that single motherhood was incredibly isolating, and very quickly, I became depressed. Times got very tough, and I ended up having to get on public assistance. Coming from a middle-class, well-educated family, having graduated from a prestigious college, traveling and experiencing the world, and being trilingual, I never imagined accepting public assistance was something I'd have to do. To stand in that line for six hours with my two-month-old with my still-sore postpartum body was extremely humbling. I was ashamed of what had become of me, which made me isolate myself even further, even from people I was trying to build community with.

I was ashamed of what had become of me, which made me isolate myself even further, even from people I was trying to build community with.

It took a while after my return to the States to get back into my healing practices. It took me restabilizing my life and going back to a well-paying, traditional career to have the calm to be present with myself again. It's very hard to be in spiritual work when your financial world feels in turmoil. There are ways to access healing connections with very limited means or no means, but it's so very hard to do that. So oddly enough, it was a return to some of the same aspects of the stable American life that I had rejected prior to Brazil that allowed me to hold space for myself and others again. It was only when I had a sound mind—achieved through getting my shit together and the peace of mind of having a steady job—that I was able to tap into my subconscious. My external world had to get right before I worked on my internal world, as ironic as that may seem.

The things that I learned about myself in all of the ceremonies and medicine work I adopted in Bahia really have allowed me to know myself, nature, and the spirit realm more deeply, beyond the illusions of our three-dimensional world. And in knowing my true essence, my true beauty, and my true purpose,

I'm able to give myself grace for my imperfections. Who I truly am is love and light and peace and universal energy. Some days I cry, wail, and moan about the weight of life, but this is the journey. The light and the shadow. The teachings I gained from living among communities of healers, being in indigenous ceremonies, and learning from the great mystics and my elders in Brazil have stayed with me. One of the biggest things they taught me is how to manage ego: ego death and submission to a higher consciousness. Applying and integrating that into my day-to-day back home has been a savior of my humility and ability to reconnect. In the end, those lessons silence any sense of shame and tell me that everything is actually okay. I am god experiencing herself, as is every living thing on this planet and perhaps beyond. I'm just honored to be on earth at this time and in this way. I'm honored to have been entrusted as a healer and teacher simply by sharing my gifts and my tools for self-liberation.

Legacy Building

Lindsey Farrar
Founder, CRWNMAG

In my early twenties, I did what I was "supposed" to do: go to school, get a good job, keep my head down… But it wasn't enough for me. I felt out of place, and that my potential was being actively stifled. After four years of corporate life, I quit and took a few months to travel through Europe—across Ireland, England, France, Italy, and Spain. Traveling solo and being left to my own devices in places where I didn't speak the language or where I could easily get lost opened up a new part of myself. I'd traveled with friends to the Caribbean a handful of times before, but this was a defining moment for me because it introduced me to my own independence. Traveling was a good pause and gave me time to take stock of my life and figure out what I wanted to do next.

When I returned to LA, I worked in a few start-ups and eventually joined one led by a woman just a year older than me as her first full-time hire. I saw up close how she was running and growing her business and how unapologetic she was about making it happen. Though I'd already dabbled in entrepreneurship myself, the experience unlocked a new understanding and permission for audacity. It reignited my entrepreneurial spirit and confirmed that I was ready to take a new leap of my own.

A couple of years passed. I moved to NYC, and Nkrumah, my then friend (turned business partner, turned husband!), and I both worked for start-ups and felt we needed more. One evening on my rooftop in Brooklyn, we conceptualized the idea of creating a premium print lifestyle publication that would use natural hair as a lens through which to engage Black women in higher thought. We saw the "natural hair movement" taking flight in the digital space, as women on YouTube and Instagram were redefining beauty standards for Black women in real time. We decided to immortalize the phenomenon— and the larger Black creative renaissance we observed—in print with *CRWNMAG*.

Our specific experiences and skill sets truly came together seamlessly… divinely. When we created a zine and put it in women's hands at a Black music festival, we saw their eyes light up. Questions and hair stories and positive energy flowed freely. We received our first preorder the very next day, before the full (140-page) magazine even existed. It struck a chord for women because there was a void at the time when it came to authentic conversations that centered on Black women's experiences. We wanted to create a magazine that we could flip through and finally see ourselves, and our beautiful range of hair textures, on every page.

When it comes to our cultural expressions, particularly around our hair—something that is without a doubt unique to *us*—we have

I want to see us do the healing work and bring our healed selves—and our precious time, talent, and resources—to the larger, collective work.

historically been leveraged for other people's benefit (read: *profit*). We've contributed to so many industries, and an unfathomable amount of money has been made off of Black women's hair and not gone back into our community. The culture needed *CRWNMAG* and had been looking for something like it for so long. While *CRWNMAG* won't resolve all of the issues of our world, it has helped to fill a gap of existential purpose. It is *ours*.

It was challenging to create something that hadn't existed before, to pursue it and maintain faith around the vision. I was tested in every way through the process of creating it and getting it out into the world. It required us to be resourceful, to stand the test. There were points along the way where we needed to push through, business-wise, because we literally had to eat. I remember feeling a lot of pressure at one point during a *cold* New York winter, caught between having orders to fill but receiving a shipment of damaged magazines. We didn't have the working capital to reprint at the time, so we had to go through a lengthy claims process with an indefinite turnaround time. I was in tears; I felt defeated and doubtful, and I questioned if we were on the right path. But Nkrumah, who was my roommate at the time, lives in an alternate reality where everything is possible. He didn't even waver for half a second

and came through with encouraging words. Surrounding yourself with people who mirror and expand your faith is so important. I definitely found that in Nkrumah, which is a reason why we're married now.

Looking back in the rearview mirror, it's overwhelming to think how much we've grown. The number of magazines that once made me question everything, we sell in a matter of a week now. Thankfully, revenue has increased every year and our partnerships have expanded. We pushed through every trial to be in the position we are in now, and we wouldn't have experienced the edification of seeing the vision through if we hadn't persisted. It goes without saying that we've come this far because of our belief in God and the belief that this is a divine purpose that has been placed in us. We see it as our duty to ensure this vision is manifested.

I think back to my twenties, when I was dabbling in different things, wandering and looking for a sense of purpose. The journey of finding that purpose in *CRWNMAG* and its impact has been a gift. I'm grateful for the alignment in our journey. There has been so much grace given to us, and so many doors have opened seemingly miraculously. The really beautiful blessings of this journey have outweighed the discouraging moments. They have served as signs that say we're on the right path. And I know we haven't even scratched the surface.

Ownership has always been very important to me. Many of us grew up having to imagine and mentally insert ourselves into white spaces, so when we do see Black faces, we're just happy to be represented at all. Being able to see ourselves in mainstream media can feel like progress, but there is far too much content *about* Black women that decodes our culture for white consumption. The way Black women are leveraged in white spaces is problematic because there's rarely diversity and depth in how we're represented; they pander to us but they're not really *for* us. They understand that our beautiful brown skin sells, but they're less interested in truly serving us. I understand why we crave even just some level of representation,

but it's even more necessary to create our own spaces, our own institutions. We have to cling to truth and set the record straight by telling our own stories from our own voices.

This starts with reprogramming our thinking. Instead of insisting on inclusion in spaces that were never meant for us, we need to invest in creating stronger Black-owned ecosystems. There's a shift in mindset that needs to happen to frame our lens of creative entrepreneurship to be more resource and business driven so that we are in positions to say no to institutions that aren't directly serving us. It's more than just "buying Black" while it's trending or "supporting" Black businesses—it's a holistic investment in Black institution building. It's an investment in our continuity and autonomy. It's a reclamation of our power—a power that we give freely to institutions that will leverage our influence and energy and sell it for the low.

This requires a collective effort, but in my mind, the reprogramming begins on an individual level. We have to take accountability for our own healing and our own growth, before we try to take on the world. Just as the system has made us doubt our value, it has undermined our sense of self as well. It makes us mistrust our brothers and sisters, making it all but impossible to build beyond ourselves. That cycle is something I am committed to helping break as part of the legacy I want to leave. I want to see us do the healing work and bring our healed selves—and our precious time, talent, and resources—to the larger, collective work. We can wait all day for a charismatic leader to come save us, but the only way that we are going to change our circumstances is if we lead ourselves.

Between Worlds

To be in the in-between feels like a balance between two or more truths, identities, or conditions. It can make you believe you aren't whole without one side or the other and have you question your sense of self and belonging, or sense of self. But the perspective that comes with betweenness can offer insight into ourselves and the world around us. Making connections between the two empowers us to be authors of our own lives.

Melded from Kin

Chloe Dulce Louvouezo

I am from my mother's wandering heart, the ambiguity of the path she walked and the permission she gave for reinvention, her belief in human dignity, and an optimism for new days. I am also from the aromatic steam rising from the boiling pots of my father's kitchen and the sounds and smells of a Congo I barely knew.

My mother, Christy, grew up in a middle-class white Northern Californian family in homes with tidy lawns and flower beds in the garden. She has always been an introvert who has enjoyed the company of herself more than of others. As a girl she would listen to vinyl Motown and opera records and imagine the story lines that shaped them, and get lost in books that took her to places she'd only imagined. On Sunday evenings she and her sister would watch *Lassie*, and over the summers she would go door-to-door selling packets of flower seeds. She was raised in a quiet household, strict and minimal. There was never any drama in her home. But there also most definitely was; it was just never spoken of. A suicide in the family left them with a quiet sadness and solemnness that seemed to paralyze connection. Affection wasn't their culture and while there was immense reverence and pride for the life path she, her sister, father, and mother followed, expression and endearment were not love languages passed down generationally.

Suffocated by the sterility of the home and the conservatism of 1960s Southern California where they'd moved, my mother immersed herself in a career of international development that would introduce her to life beyond

the manicured lawns. She was soft-spoken yet sharp and thoughtful. She was artistic and had wanderlust, with dreams of experiences outside the country. When I was a child, she introduced me to a world of creating and exploring. When we lived in the States, we spent weekends at bagel shops, Smithsonian museums, and botanical gardens. In the evenings, I watched her curled up on the couch drawing charcoal sketches of wooden benches and grass huts. Her business suits were lined with printed and indigo-dyed wax cloth. The dinner parties she hosted with friends from the African diaspora filled our studio apartment with echoes of banter in Franglais, a resonance of franco-phone West Africa that migrated with her wherever we moved. I grew up intrigued to uncover the mystery of who my mother was and

how she came to be. I learned more about her through her love affair with Niger—where she found her strongest footing and belonging—than through anything else. The wooden and straw masks that embellished our studio walls and the Pan-African books that lined our bookshelves told stories of her past and the life she still desired ahead.

In contrast, my father, M'bayero, was a spirited man. In his earlier days he was a lead dancer in the National Congolese Dance Troupe. While his brothers and sisters stayed behind in Brazzaville, where opportunities were rare and dreams were washed away with the equatorial rain, my father traveled the world, from Russia to China to Brazil and across Europe, to perform. In his twenties, he traveled across the Pacific Ocean from Algeria to Cuba by boat with seventeen dance group delegations from different countries across Africa.

The stage channeled his command, vibrance, and charisma, and they come through in every photo archiving his past. He had a loyal relationship with rhythm; it lifted him to another world and made him feel big and notable. After migrating to America, that validation meant something. It was the one thing I admired in him—a purity in connection to his art.

But my memories of my father were not all charming. My first is of frantic cries coming from my parents' bedroom in our Pasadena apartment. I was three years old. I pushed the door open and stood in the doorway to see my mother on the bed and my father standing at the foot gripping a belt tightly at each end. There was the other time my father swung a full wine bottle over my mother's head in front of company. And there were other times after that. His abuse permeated our household. There was a tension that lingered in the air, waiting for him to crack at any moment. My mother and I soon left to move to the East Coast, and later to Niger, far outside of his reach. I would take sporadic visits with my mother to see him in Oakland,

where he had settled down. Despite the painful reminders our relationship triggered, my rapport with him was my only liaison with the Congolese culture. If only to feel closer to the culture, I convinced myself that a relationship, however toxic, was worth maintaining at the time.

I have balanced both the attachment and distance of being Congolese American. I was never close to either side of my family and often felt out of place. Within my mother's family, I was always the only person of color. My grandparents hosted holiday dinners and were the pillars of our American home base when we would visit from abroad. No one else in the pews of their Protestant church or the neighborhood of their hilly street had coils in their hair or as much melanin in their skin. The interactions I witnessed my mother's parents having with people of color were in their volunteer service and veterans circles. Few affirma-

tions told me that I fit within their whiteness. And while being American felt tangible and experienced to me, the unfamiliarity of Congo also felt amiss in its own way. I'd barely touched its dirt or spoke its language and had never met two of my three sisters, creating a sometimes equally foreign impression of family and home.

Though I was a stranger to Congo, an alliance with the country and the stories of it still lived deep within me. I was five years old the last time I visited Brazzaville, and I held tightly to the memories of that trip. I remember being welcomed at the airport by aunts, uncles, and cousins who threw me on their shoulders and paraded my father and me to the parking lot, chanting songs of rejoicing. I felt embraced by *my people*, and that trip cemented a reminiscence of young memories. In the mornings my cousins and I filled our plastic buckets with cold water and bathed ourselves in the front yard. The days were spent playing foosball on the outdoor patio and piling into taxis heading across town to the market to buy cassava roots and beans. In the evenings I cooked plantains with my half sister and sold them to pedestrians at the side of the dirt road near our house. We'd collect the change we earned for the night and deliver it to our grandmother, who taught me to wrap batik cloth around my waist and to pee in recycled soup cans in the corner of the bedroom at night.

I would think back on that trip fondly as the only remains I had of memories of my kin. Growing up, I fantasized about an intimate relationship with my Congolese brother and sisters. I'd wonder where they were and how they were doing, but the ocean between us made us such distant strangers. And our distance—them in Brazzaville, me in my travels to Niger, the United States, and places in between—was a reminder that our lives were disparate. Though I was born in Kinshasa, Zaire, I was born an American citizen, and the birthrights that granted divided us.

Back in California, where my father lived since migrating to the States, M'bayero and his extended Congolese friends and family were a microcosm of Congolese culture. He taught Sunday dance classes at the Malonga Casquelourd Center for the Arts in Oakland, named after my late uncle. While my uncles pounded down on the djembe drums between their legs, sweat soaking their shorts and glistening across their bare chests, M'bayero led a full class of men and women through intricate footsteps, loose hip twists, and vibrant laughter. I'd sit quietly in a chair against the wall, watching his command of the room. High from the exhilaration, his students would trickle out of the studio after class with good vibes, high fives, and promises of returning the following week. After class, we'd

> I was looking to him to heal one area of identity while another was still an open sore.

gather at an uncle's apartment to hover over bowls of fufu dripping with peanut sauce.

In my late twenties, though, I realized that using my father as my liaison with my Congolese identity had become convoluted with the resentment of him that I hadn't yet dealt with. I was looking to him to heal one area of identity while another was still an open sore. When I understood that correlation, I made a decision to compartmentalize the two. I resolved to be intentional about forging a relationship and connection with Congo outside of the linkage my father provided. It had been twenty-five years since I had last visited Brazzaville. I returned for my thirtieth birthday, hoping this would be a homecoming that would close the loop on my kinship with my family. I wondered if the memories I savored from all those years ago would be just as meaningful to them. I wondered if visiting would root my diaspora wandering that never found its home.

Again I was met at the airport with chants from my family, reverberated by claps and slaps of kisses on my cheek. But the drive home revealed that we were not picking up where we left off. The cousins I once knew as children were now adults with children and worries of their own, and the aunts and uncles I remembered as boisterous and cheery were now fatigued. The weight of stress, from little opportunity and resources, during our time apart showed in the way they asked about my life in America; their inferences suggesting an American Dream out of their reach. On that trip I fell in love with the daughter of my younger sister who had passed away several years before and the daughter of my older sister who still shares my father's dimples with me.

There was a magnetism between my nieces and me—an immediate harmony. "Take them with you," my sister asked the day before I left Brazzaville. "There is nothing for them here." My family's desire for a life outside of Congo meant they, too, were living in the in-between: between where they were and where they dreamed to be, as so many of us are, and I was their bridge. What I've learned from teetering between both sides of my family is how complicated and layered family is, as a structure and concept meant to ground us in who we are and how we navigate this world. I've had to leave space for the role of family to evolve. In longing for my family to be what it had never been—an anchoring in belonging—I came to learn that that was what I could be for them.

Twice of Everything

Nneka Julia
Writer, Photographer, and Storyteller

Storytelling is in my blood. As early as I can remember, I would sit at my father's feet while he read me stories from tattered papers from his library about the tortoise and the animal kingdom in Igbo land. I had an uncle who passed away recently whom they called the ogoro tree, named after the tall palm trees grown in West Africa. Everyone in the community mourned his passing, largely because of the stories that died with him. Without archiving, an entire generation can die. It has, it does, and it will. My father documented his life through photos and preserved so many memories so well. Candid shots at family functions, christenings, barbecues, weddings, vacations, and a host of beautiful and stylish self-portraits. Looking at these old photos made me ask, "Am I documenting my life the way it should be documented?" My dad was always big on this Jim Rohn quote: "There are three things to leave behind: your photographs, your library, and your personal journals. These things are certainly going to be more valuable to future generations than your furniture!" He has been intentionally curating and cultivating all three things.

That led me to pick up a camera. When I returned to Cambodia for the first time in thirteen years, I brought my camera with me and never put it down. Ever since I can remember, I was the kid who painted on the walls.

Anything and everything was my canvas. But this time, photography, for me, was the paint. Photos were the brush to color my world at the time. It became something I was positively obsessed with. I love seeing the beautiful parts of every place as much as the nuance, the yin to the yang. Light doesn't exist without the darkness. I want to tell stories in a way that takes audiences to the places I've been and shares the lessons I've learned through the people I meet. I want to create an archive of understanding. In our now-digital age, storytelling is the impact I want to leave behind, so that my family and our greater community can pull from these stories.

My story starts with my parents. They met in Washington, DC, in the 1980s at a telecommunications company named Denro. My father was hired as a technician, my mom was doing clerical work. My father was met with many nos before finally getting a yes. Both were survivors of their countries' genocides— my father from Nigeria where the Biafran War consumed the late 1960s, and my mother from Cambodia where they experienced genocide in the late 1970s. When they met, their worlds collided and the creation of our family came from the blending of their cultures. They raised us in Pennsylvania, in a household where two languages were always being yelled on the phone. There was a melting pot of different

No human being goes through this life unscathed or untouched by an experience that forcefully demands that we pause, that we reflect, that we change.

spices and foods, shared family values, and a culture of oneness. Fried rice and soup porridge (babaw) on Mondays. Jollof and fufu on Fridays. Both parents believed "it takes a village," "no one has two heads" (so sit close to the classmates who get A's), "respect your elders," and "never forget your roots." Somehow, my parents managed America without the need to refer to the typical village life they would have otherwise leaned on back home. Nevertheless, they instilled and inculcated a sense of togetherness within our insular family.

My parents didn't mention genocide much when I was growing up. I had no idea they'd both lived through it until a few years ago when I asked them to record their stories for later generations. My dad had spoken to me about losing a recording of my late grandmother's voice in a house fire. I started thinking about how amazing it would be to hear my grandparents' take on love, life, loss, and everything in between. I started recording them for future generations for the sake of archiving. Now, I plan on using the transcriptions of their stories for a future book and screenplay.

I didn't know my dad had fought in the Nigerian-Biafran War. I didn't know my mother took a three-month trek through Thailand to get to the border of Cambodia. I just knew that they'd escaped, as they had to have gotten to

America somehow. I never got the full stories until I was in my early twenties, because when I would ask about their pasts when I was younger, they only told me the versions they wanted me to hear. But now that I know their stories, I see the effect each genocide had on their parenting. My mother is an extremely frugal Southeast Asian woman. It doesn't matter how much money she has in the bank, no grain of rice goes to waste. That's how she and her family survived during the genocide. Cambodian civilians were put in work camps, starved, worked to death, and killed, particularly those who were educated. My grandmother had to ration very limited amounts of food for over ten family members during those times, and it became ingrained in my mother to live in scarcity. And in learning more of my father's story of living through the Biafran War, I understood the roots of his sense of pure leadership. At the age of fifteen, he willingly signed up to join the war as a soldier. He learned leadership from top generals as they confronted death across enemy lines.

In middle school, I switched from a public school to a private Catholic school, and I was one of three Black kids there. The feeling of what it's like to be Black in America was something my parents had never experienced. It's something I still need to explain to them to this day: what it was like being a Black kid

in a primarily white school, being fed into the public-school system as a high schooler, being among peers who didn't understand that Blackness is a spectrum. I am a bridge between two races in my family; my experience of race also differs vastly when I visit Cambodia and Nigeria, both presenting such a paradigm shift from my life in America. When I visit my dad's village in Nigeria, they call me a white person, or an *oyinbo*. It's not based on color, but on privilege, access, language, and culture. Your identity there is less about Blackness and more conscious of your Americanness. In Cambodia, my Blackness can be confusing to my family and their community. They look at me and they don't get it. Like everywhere in the world, colorism shapes people's perceptions. Light is right, bright, and beautiful; and the darker you

are, the longer you've been enslaved in the sun. But when my multiculturalism is explained to them—usually by my aunts or cousins to strangers in public or at the market, there's nothing but love and acceptance. It is family.

Before, home to me was the house that my parents resided in in Ann Arbor, Michigan. Now, coming home to myself is a state of mind. It is not treating my feelings as if they're old friends. If a guest knocks on your door, you wouldn't tell them to get off your porch with a shotgun. You would welcome them, you would feed them, you would house them for a little bit before they go to their next destination. That has been my way of coming home to myself over the past few years. No human being goes through this life unscathed or untouched by an experience that forcefully demands that we pause, that we reflect, that we change. It's honest, unabbreviated stories that have the power to build a bridge. The stories that illustrate the tenacity of opposites and the endless battles of coming face-to-face with our former selves. When you share your story, even if it's with one person, you're guiding them over the sacred bridge of understanding. Coming home to myself is about accepting all of my former selves, accepting my emotions, and accepting my feelings, because they can either serve or master—they can either control you or you can control them. It's realizing that I have a place anywhere I choose because I myself am home.

Beyond the In-Between

Elaine Welteroth
Author and Journalist

Black womanhood has come to define much of my journey. It has bloomed over time, starting with the seeds my mother planted. She is a very proud Black woman who was raised with the same pride she instilled in us: pride that was rooted in the Black church, in gospel music, in soul food, in the expansive range of our hairstyles.

She is the kind of Black woman who never anticipated falling in love with a white man, let alone the rock-guitar-playing, hippie-spirited, blue-eyed, cowboy-hat-wearing man who would become my father.

The cultures on either side of my family are starkly different. Growing up, there were elements of both that I gravitated toward, and others that repelled me.

Holidays in my early life were spent with my dad's side of the family in Northern California where we were raised in a predominantly white, middle-class American bubble. Our time together felt friendly, polite. Everyone played nice, but there were invisible barriers we all intuitively understood and operated within, never daring to explore each other beyond the small talk and smiles. We were always welcomed with open arms and hearts. Yet in their company, I found myself sitting up a little bit

Black culture,
Black women, and
my own Blackness
have become
my safe havens.

straighter, smiling a little bit longer and harder than felt natural, more in breaths than exhales. I yearned for the ease of just being, but it never fully seemed to come.

Early on, my mother's best friend and her children became our Black "play" family, deepening my definition of family. Our time together always excited my senses. Their company felt warm and sweet like the scent of candied yams that filled the air. We'd play games, we'd squabble, we'd laugh so hard our bellies ached. The space was so full of words, yours might have to fight for airtime. Sometimes there were arguments at the table and things got a little rowdy. But in the chaos, I felt more at ease, like I could let my hair down. I leaned in more. I laughed louder. I was at home.

But the sticky summer I spent in the South being introduced to our Black blood relatives was among both the more grounding and jarring experiences of my childhood. It was the first time I was called a "white girl" and made to feel somehow "other" among my own. My punk-rock brother and I didn't check the boxes of Blackness they immediately recognized, and so our search for belonging in Black spaces came up short.

This trend continued through college. Until then, I had found a shelter of psychological safety in the company of white friends.

We spoke alike. We dressed alike. And we came dangerously close to believing those similarities added up to true belonging.

Being mixed race in America is to exist on an inherent and perpetual spectrum of "otherness." You are both, and, but also not quite fully, one or the other. You are often caught somewhere among the world's perceptions of where you land between white and Black, and your own feelings about the space you occupy. When surrounded by your own white family and friends, you feel different. When surrounded by your own Black family and friends, you still feel different. And, like chameleons, we learn to become adept at sliding along that spectrum as our environments shift. Or as our sense of safety within those environments shifts.

It was ultimately being called the N-word in college that offered a sobering turning point toward a much deeper exploration of what it actually means to be Black in America. This was a journey not one of my white friends could go on with me. Nor could they relate. That thin veil of sameness we shared over the years disappeared in an instant when that word sliced right through me. You can never unhear it. You can never unfeel it. It robbed me of the illusion that there was ever any option to choose what side I was on. Distrust replaced the naivete I had once carried around about my own racial identity.

The invalidating experience of being othered by your own and rejected by the majority is something most Black woman can relate to, biracial or not. Whatever the spectrum—race, gender, sexuality, ability, or class—on some level, we've all longed for a sense of belonging at times and in spaces where it wasn't extended to us. We do a disservice to our collective sisterhood and brotherhood when we categorize each other according to society's expectations or stereotypes that force us into ill-fitting, cookie-cutter boxes of what we think Black should look like.

My immersion into the Black community came from a place of seeking protection, solidarity, and safety from white environments. And it continued after college as I moved to New York City to work at *Ebony* magazine. I went to a Black church in Harlem. I spent weekends with my newfound Black sister-friends. The world that I was building for myself was one that centered on Blackness. Because that's what felt like home. Starting my career at a Black magazine informed who I am professionally and the responsibility that I take with me into every white space I enter. It also deepened my relationships with Black women. There's a certain unspoken, indescribable sisterhood among Black women that makes me feel safe and seen and intuitively understood. I have found so much comfort in that sisterhood.

Black culture, Black women, and my own Blackness have become my safe havens.

Every single day in America, Black women and people of color are marginalized, overlooked, underpaid, and underestimated—as we have been for generations. When that happens, survival instincts will ask us to conform because of inherited generational trauma that has taught us we are not good enough in our natural state. But the spaces we create for each other offer an opportunity to rewire our minds and our spirits to exist fully and to believe that we are more than enough, even against the odds. To defy those odds is a true act of rebellion. It creates new ways of being and sets examples of what Black female liberation looks like, not just for ourselves, but for other Black women and for the generations of Black women that follow.

Manifesting
Through Aspiration

Meryanne Loum-Martin
Owner, Jnane Tamsna

I did not plan my life the way it unfolded. One thing led to another. But at each step, I put all my energy to optimize the direction it was moving toward. Since I was a child, I knew that I was brought here to build. My parents loved traveling, and by the age of twelve, I had seen more countries than most adults. I was always making sketches of how I would change and redesign places, rooms, or houses. At a very young age, I decided that I would eventually become an architect. It became an obsession. At the age of thirteen, I had subscriptions to all the architecture magazines available. I went to architecture school after passing my French baccalaureate at sixteen years old. Architecture studies were going extremely well until my third year at École Nationale Supérieure des Beaux-Arts in Paris when I needed credits in math and physics, and I couldn't keep up. So, I withdrew and went to law school instead, following the footsteps of many lawyers on both sides of my family. When I realized that I wasn't going to become an architect, I fell into depression. My whole world felt like it was crumbling; the idea of not doing what I truly wanted to do ate me up.

My mother was from the French West Indies and my father is from Senegal. I was born in Ivory Coast, but my parents raised me in Paris. Our family always had this idea to one day have a family vacation home abroad, which could not be farther than three hours from our home base in Paris. Because of my passion for architecture and design, I took the initiative of finding our vacation home. Back then, I had heard wonderful things about Morocco and its culture. I lived in Paris, where Yves Saint Laurent was such an icon that everyone knew he adored Marrakech. Since his taste was legendary, I was very much influenced by his choice and thought this must be the perfect place for our cosmopolitan family. I was very lucky that a Parisian friend of mine was part of the circle "who put Marrakech on the map." When I came to Marrakech for the first time in December 1985 to look for land, it was love at first sight. From the moment I stepped foot on the tarmac, I knew this place was going to forever change my life. Thanks to my friend, I had the rare opportunity to live the private Marrakech life and understand why the city was quickly becoming a legend.

I soon found a piece of land. Four weeks later, I came back with my parents, and they also loved it and immediately bought it. They gave me carte blanche to build and design what we thought would only be a family holiday home at the time. It was an abandoned site with just four concrete walls and no ceiling. Although I was a Parisian lawyer then with my architecture studies far behind me, my determination and passion for all things architecture were still intact. I had found the canvas that would allow me to return to my first love.

What started as a family vacation home evolved into the launch of a boutique villa rental service, a place where visitors could experience Marrakech in an intimate and stylish way. As the villa was beautiful and guaranteed absolute privacy, it soon hosted celebrities and royalty from around the world. Blending five-star service, unique experiences and surprises, impeccable food, and access to exclusive adventures made this property world famous. Between 1990 and 2000, the property was featured everywhere from *Vogue* to *Architectural Digest, New York Times, Wall Street Journal, Forbes*, and more. As our guests would say, "very famous to very few," it went on to win the "Best private villa in the world" award from *Harper's & Queen* in 2000.

After years of back and forth between practicing law in Paris and overseeing construction of the villas' expansion in Morocco, I left the Bar and focused on the Marrakech properties' marketing full-time. In 1995, Paris was paralyzed by strikes so my husband and I decided to leave the city for good. The next summer, we moved to Marrakech and have been here ever since. My Parisian friends thought that I was out of my mind for leaving law and moving to an Arab country as a Black woman. But as I had always been a minority everywhere, I never considered this an impossible challenge. I was ready to explore the possibilities life would bring. I needed change. We wanted space, nature, and a more creative family life than what Paris could offer.

Marrakech is absolutely fascinating. Its influences intersect so many cultures, from Arab, Berber, sub-Saharan Africa, to colonial art deco. While living in full-speed modernity, its identity remains resilient, its cultural heritage is untouched and protected, and its craftsmanship is in its ability to build or design exactly the same things that have been passed from fathers to sons for centuries. The culture is one of its own, and I had to quickly learn the new context that surrounded me. I had always been fully in charge of my parents' projects, where the workers knew only me. But when my husband and I decided to create our own project in 2001, my learning curve with gender and race was tested. The construction trade in Marrakech, as in most places, is a male-dominated world. The workers were not used to being told what to do by a woman. In Paris, I took my ability to advocate for myself for granted, particularly as a lawyer, whereas in Marrakech, I found myself needing to impose my voice much more. I spoke up in such a way that didn't leave any margin for negotiation so that I couldn't be taken advantage of. This was, for the most part, unheard of for a Black woman in the country at the time. I cannot say it was always easy, but it was always worth the fight.

My American husband would tell me that he was ashamed of the way I spoke to workers at the construction site. It only amplified the difference between how respect is earned between a Black woman and a white man in a male-dominated world. I would tell him, "Yes, of course. You with your blue eyes and soft voice, workers will follow your instructions. As an African woman, if I don't speak constantly with authority, nothing moves." Depending on the trade I am dealing with, I have to adapt. When I feel that being a woman, and particularly a Black woman, is no issue, I can be diplomatic, flexible, and attentive. When I need to get things done and have a specific idea in mind, then it is key to express that there is no space for discussion. If people are uncomfortable with us Black women holding positions they're not used to seeing us in, that is their problem. I've already moved forward. As long as we deliver, what more is there to say? Marrakech is a small town, and craftsmen now know that it is a waste of time to try to play around with the work I expect.

Standing up for my ideas in a male-dominated culture isn't new to me; activism runs in my blood as family members have stood up for important social and political causes for generations. My last surviving aunt would tell me about our lineage of dreamers. When slavery was abolished in the West Indies, so many former enslaved people did not want to work in agriculture anymore because it was too painful of a reminder. But one of my ancestors, confident that his skill in farming was his ticket to upward mobility, invested his livelihood as a free man in agriculture and land ownership. In his lifetime, his son—my great-grandfather— became a lawyer, moved to France, was elected to the French Congress, befriended W. E. B. Du Bois, and organized the first Pan-African Congress in 1919. Our ancestor born enslaved and freed in 1848 created an opportunity for generational wealth, and it is through this passed-down inheritance that I was able to purchase my land in Morocco and pursue my own dreams. I think of it as one man's aspirations opening doors for future generations. And we are where

I spoke up in such a way that didn't leave any margin for negotiation so that I couldn't be taken advantage of. This was, for the most part, unheard of for a Black woman in the country at the time.

we are today because of all of our phenomenal ancestors who paved the way. Black history is full of examples of men and women who never took no for an answer and who believed nothing was impossible. That is how I want to show up in this world.

Yes, it might seem crazy that a successful Parisian lawyer left it all to live her dream of designing and building villas in a country so different from her own, but we owe it to ourselves and to our communities not only to aspire and to achieve the impossible, but to passionately pursue our dreams if we are lucky to have them. Our dreams are fragile, and having too many untapped dreams, can be damaging to our spirit. It's easy for dreams to crumble when we don't believe they'll ever be manifested. At some point you have to ask yourself, what are you willing to do to get what you want from life? It's one thing to be a dreamer, but to be a dreamer *and* an executor, that takes a drizzle of madness and a ton of determination.

Saudade

Lili Lopez
Artist

I am from Senegal and Cape Verde, but I grew up in Paris. I had a career in marketing, business, and media and was doing well at a creative agency. But I had a yearning to travel, to explore and experience life in a way I never had before.

I was ambitious in my career but realized that it was not fulfilling me. I was on the search for a different type of accomplishment and fulfillment. Paris felt too small. I wanted more than it could offer. I traveled to West Africa and offered to work as a photojournalist and later as a foster mother with a humanitarian organization for five months, but when I returned to Paris, I knew I had outgrown the city. The job market was stagnant, and I started to feel stuck and uninspired. I decided to change my scenery, so I packed my bags and moved to New York City, the supposed land of opportunity. The move was more motivated by the urge to leave the staleness of Paris than it was to chase the glitter of New York.

It was the first time I had been to the Big Apple. As soon as I landed, I was energized by the city, and I instinctively felt like it was where I needed to be. After a three-month trial period, I chose to stay in New York as a leap of faith. I really trusted that it would lead me to where I needed to be, and I trusted that everything would fall into place.

I loved the newness that New York brought to my life. I was excited by the unknown, by the fact that I had so much to learn, and by the idea that getting to know new people would force me into new spaces. New York was feeding me in this way. But the reality hit me shortly after. Visa challenges and living in an "undocumented" box, which altered how some people viewed and treated me and inhibited my ability to return home to my family, affected me mentally and emotionally. Having traveled and lived in Africa and Europe, I had been exposed to different ways of living. The United States was completely different in yet another way. I struggled with translating myself through the language barrier and cultural disconnect.

Having to navigate this new world on my own, I felt extremely vulnerable and went from feeling truly liberated as I discovered the streets and the momentum of New York to losing parts of myself. I didn't fit the codes of those segments of New York culture that felt superficial. The transactional nature of some relationships was a barrier to genuine relationships. Trying to fit in rather than be who I am was painfully uncomfortable. I found myself trusting less and isolating more to protect myself from the harshness of the city. I became resentful of the hype around the American Dream, which can be a disservice to the reality of many immigrants. Without connection and a solid support system, it is a false perception. And sometimes the American Dream can turn into a nightmare.

I thought everything would fall into place. And I assure you, it did; it was just a very hard and lonely road to get there. I stayed because I had already sacrificed so much in being away from my family and loved ones, and I felt like I couldn't return until I made my time away

You know you are living in authenticity when you are not betraying your intentions.

worth it. I was committed to get to a point where I could finally smile at New York again.

I started drawing and painting as therapy, and I became an artist, which was never the plan. People reacted well to my art, and I've been doing art in many mediums ever since, from illustrations and paintings to visual storytelling. Every time I create something, I stay still for a second and observe my canvas. I reflect on it. I analyze the different aspects of my aesthetic and my work to better understand myself. Like my artistry, which is my language of emotional and intuitive exploration, self-discovery has been the basis of my New York experience. I'm into knowing who I am fully and want to always explore it. I never want to betray that. New York straightened and sharpened my analysis of myself by helping me understand my own wars within. Leaning into my artistry was by necessity, but it has

The more I understand myself, the more I relate the idea of home not to a place but to a feeling of being understood.

pushed me to understand my limits in compromising myself.

When I think of my relationship with New York, so much distrust has come from the ways in which the city has challenged me. But my love for the city has been in also appreciating how it has forced me to connect with myself more despite the friction. It has brought me opportunities I never thought I could have. It made me do things I never thought I could do. It has shown me how resourceful we can be in moments of challenge. It has put on my path awesome individuals who have inspired me with their humanity. It has shown me how the world needs more empathy, curiosity, and understanding. It has made me even more sensitive to the story of immigrants and what it truly means to leave home for the unknown. It has deepened my relationships with my mother by helping me see her as a woman in the ways she was there for me in moments of doubt. My wins were her wins, my challenges were hers. The way she held my hand through it all humanized her and gave me insight into the why of who she is today that only our distance could reveal.

The more I understand myself, the more I relate the idea of home not to a place but to a feeling of being understood—beyond the titles or what society tells us we are and beyond the accolades or accomplishments. It's been therapeutic for me to rip down those fake layers that we put on just to survive and stay relevant. Being ourselves fully requires us to strip away what we think represents success and instead self-examine how we're showing up in the world and evolving through the trials. It starts with aligning our actions with our intentions. You know you are living in authenticity when you are not betraying your intentions. This requires us to be honest, with ourselves and with others, by confessing and critiquing our truth. We all have mirrors around us that reflect what is missing from our lives that, if we just dare to look into them, can shift our perspective of ourselves and our circumstances.

ma douceur est ma force

PART II
BEAR WITNESS

Still I Rise

Sometimes it's easier to operate from the wounds of our experiences than to conjure up the faith that there is more beauty to this life than the past might suggest. We owe it to ourselves to give our stories a chance to be free from the chains that hold them captive from healing. It takes some time to redefine what we think those wounds say about the women we are. Despite the trauma, despite how we felt about ourselves yesterday, and despite sometimes feeling bound to our past, how do we rewrite our personal story as one of resilience and reframe our interpretation of it while still coping with the bread crumbs it leaves behind?

A Pierced Memory Imagined

Chloe Dulce Louvouezo

I sat on the edge of my father's bed in his small five-hundred-square-foot studio apartment in Oakland. The beat of Papa Wemba playing from the 1990s stereo cassette system that hummed in the background had been the soundtrack to nearly every memory I held from that apartment. I adjusted myself on the corner of the mattress and smoothed down the bedsheets adorned with images of large green dollar bills. For as long as I could remember, some version of those sheets were his staple decor. The Benjamins represented his aspiration for the American Dream.

Every detail of the apartment had always been familiar but uncomfortable to me—the stale smell of cologne that permeated the air, the thick years-old layer of dust that blanketed the blinds, and the Catholic beads draped over the embellished shrine dedicated to my late Congolese grandparents. Their portraits stared blankly at me. I scanned the framed photos of my father that lined the wall. The candid shots captured his thirty-year-old frame in dance— arms stretched, feet and hips pulling his body in opposite directions—suited in full grass skirts and cowrie shell ankle bracelets. As Papa

> **To me, it meant bringing my healing full circle by being awake through triggering experiences without allowing them to haunt me all over again.**

Wemba's music played on, I could feel those images come to life. This is how I wish I remembered my father.

I visited his studio on and off throughout my childhood. But this visit was different. This time, my son Myel was with us for the first time. Part of me wanted to test their interaction and see what knee-jerk reaction would arise in me. At eighteen months old, he climbed across the carpet and onto the futon and plopped down into the pillows. The three of us share the same nose, chin, eyes, and dimples—my father, my son, and I. And we share a family history that over time chipped away at my sense of self and became the catalyst for both my pain and my breakthrough. It was hard to imagine that I could be sitting next to my father again, but there I was, willing to give him a chance at vindication.

My father sat next to Myel, and they smiled at each other as he handed him a pint-size drum he'd brought from Congo. This was their first time meeting, and the drum was my father's first peace offering. As they broke the ice, I sat on the bed and watched. The nostalgic feelings were soon replaced by a sharp twist in my stomach. A cloud hovered over the lightness. I was sharing my gift with my curse.

In that moment I was taken back to when I was fifteen years old, when I vividly remember

my own light dimming. I was a tenth grader in boarding school in Tacoma, and the residential hallways buzzed with excitement as we neared the upcoming Thanksgiving break. As all of the other girls made plans to visit with family across the country, I also tried to make my own. My options were limited, having moved across the world alone from Niger to the United States and without close family nearby. I'd had an inconsistent relationship with my father for most of my life because of culture clashes and unmet expectations, but visiting him in Oakland for the break was my last resort and the rare chance to see my Oakland cousins. But those plans changed when, over a call, my mother shared news that would trigger a paradigm shift in my relationship with my father, men, and myself.

My mother told me what she had kept to herself for years: that as an infant and toddler, before my memory could recall, my own father molested me over time. Followed by a loud silence. The conversation ended shortly after. I stood in my dorm room numb. My feet were cemented to the ground, and my chest sunk in. I closed my eyes and let the phone drop to the floor, dangling by its spiral cord across my dresser. A hole was carved out of me that day. In the days, weeks, months, and years that followed, I felt cheated by how this news wove itself into my story unexpectedly. It made me feel dirty and forever stained by a truth that I would now have to live with. I couldn't separate the thought of what happened to me from what it said about me.

The news had jarring effects. It pulled me into a consciousness of inadequacy that took more than half of my life to dismantle. I had little direction on how to channel the insecurities this new truth festered. I let the shame of sexual abuse linger and lurk around corners, waiting for me to one day address. A dichotomy of perfectionism and escapism as ways to cope distracted me from being present enough to process it for years. I set an achievement bar for myself that was so high it was impossible to operate outside of imposter syndrome. I translated shame into the hope that if I just masked my imperfections with perfection, it would distract the world from knowing what had happened to me, which I had quickly internalized as part of who I was. I needed to prove to myself that I wasn't broken—a mindset driven by paranoia of my secret being discovered and judged. Being strong meant living under a veil of stoicism.

When I wasn't "on," I turned to drugs, sex, and alcohol to numb creeping thoughts. To numb ourselves is to hide, if only for a while, from the truth. I think I unknowingly wanted to create a different kind of relationship with sex, one that I alone could command. Promiscuous choices of boys at least felt like choices. Self-destructive behaviors that led to blackouts, arrests, and the wrong crowds got bad enough to jolt me into realizing I was processing unresolved pain in ways that weren't reflective of who I really was. Forgiveness of my father and of myself took its time but was later my saving grace.

Seventeen years after that day on the phone, I watched my father's attempts to connect with his grandson in his studio apartment. I sat on the edge of his bed, reminded to never get too comfortable with his presence. Myel sat there enjoying his new drum in toddler euphoria. He was the same age I was at the time of my own abuse and I wondered what, if anything, that moment meant to my father. To me, it meant bringing my healing full circle by being awake through triggering experiences without allowing them to haunt me all over again. I was removing the bullet that had pierced my being.

Healing Through Joy

Deun Ivory
Founder, the body: a home for love

My story of sexual abuse started when I was very young. I had multiple experiences with men in my family. Cousins and uncles would touch me inappropriately or dry hump me. Then, my mom was in a long-term relationship with a man who became a father figure to me. In middle school, things just got strange. My mother, who was pregnant at the time with his child, worked evenings, so after school, it was just my stepdad and me at home. He would do what he could to get close to me and touch me. He eventually started giving me money, to ease the guilt of molesting me, I assume. I didn't tell anybody because he told me not to. It was our little secret.

It was absolutely excruciating. It got to the point where I would come home from school and go straight to my room and pretend to be asleep until my mother got home. He was also abusive to her, so I didn't share my secret with her out of protectiveness. I didn't want a commotion that would cause him to beat her, and because he was the breadwinner, I worried that if he left, my family would go without money and food. It's when I went to college that I was saved. I prayed harder than I'd ever prayed in my life for God to give me the strength to say something. By then, it felt like all of my power had been taken away from me. I felt like I had

nothing; nothing to give and nothing to say and that I was worthless. When I did tell my mother, she went ballistic. She believed me and confronted him about it. He moved out shortly after, but the next year, I found out they had gotten back together. We didn't have a discus-

> There's so much beauty and joy that God wants us to access. We can't do that if we don't access pain.

sion about it. I came home from college one summer and I had to be under the same roof as the man who abused me. I didn't say anything, which created a norm of detachment.

For so long I was detached from the truth of it happening to me. I created a whole life where I became a master of compartmentalization and of dissociation. I would share my story but wouldn't insert myself into the narrative. Everyone has different ways of processing their trauma. We make sadness and silence long-term companions, not knowing that they rob us of so much, because there's so much beauty and joy that God wants us to access. We can't do that if we don't access pain. When we bury the pain, we're only harming ourselves. In order for me to cultivate self-love and treat myself with care and support, I had to give myself space to release. I had to come face-to-face with my story, to be completely healed from it. It was by conviction and a desire to finally sit with the reality of what

I want to shift culture around how Black women heal from sexual trauma by inviting them to be vulnerable, share their stories, and journey back to their bodies as safe spaces.

I had gone through that I was able to move past it. I realized I was making trauma-informed decisions based on fear and a sense of powerlessness instead of joy-filled decisions. I couldn't allow my subconscious to rule anymore; I had to get in front of the truth and sit with it.

I started my organization the body: a home for love in 2018 as an affirmation for self. It's a reminder that our body, our earth home, is a place meant for love. It was made from love and to be loved. I want to shift culture around how Black women heal from sexual trauma by inviting them to be vulnerable, share their stories, and journey back to their bodies as safe spaces. We walk alongside them on their journey of healing. Using art, creativity, dialogue, and design—from spatial design to graphic design to illustration design—as mechanisms for healing is new. As a multidisciplinary artist, I am expanding what wellness looks like for Black women. I launched the organization with support from a grant for creators who empower marginalized communities through art. I decided to use the opportunity to travel around the world for six months to interview fifteen Black women about their experiences with sexual abuse. It shifted my entire world. When I was committing myself to the six months of interviewing and photographing them, I couldn't run anymore. I couldn't build trust with them and ask them to reveal themselves to me if I wasn't willing to deal with my own truth. It was one of the hardest six months I'd ever been through because I had dissociated from my abuse for so long. It was also one of the most rewarding and healing experiences. It helped me realize that my story is bigger than me, and there is a community of women open to receiving it as much as I am open to receiving theirs. I hate that it happened to me but also know that by sharing my truth and standing in it, it empowers other women to do the same. And this brings me joy.

The name of the organization was intentional. *Home* is a safe place where you decide who and what has access to it. It's a sacred space where you have total agency. Journeying back to your body as a home for love is getting back to its initial purpose. It's an awareness of what your body really needs, what it's made for, and why you're here. It's being mindful about the energy and the aura your body feels in certain contexts, whether safe or fearful. It's an intuitiveness, joy, and agency that I want all Black women to access. Yet, when we think about Black women's experiences, it's hard for us to abide our bodies as such because for so long we've been hypersexualized. We've been indoctrinated with a narrative that we are here for the entertainment of men or we do things for the male gaze. We're demonized for how beautiful we are or how shapely we are, at an early age. It makes young girls and women feel like we're the ones who bring the unwanted attention. Society perpetuates blame on women and fails to talk about men and their wrongdoing. I want to empower and educate women on the impact of patriarchy in their own stories and instill in them that their trauma is not their fault. Rarely are Black women ever seen as innocent or given the opportunity to share our stories without being met with judgment. It saddens me that we're given this earth home

that we can't fully enjoy because others claim our bodies for themselves. Black and brown women are so beautiful. We deserve to have beautiful experiences.

I've learned how to cope and process my pain through creating. Art was always a relief, but it took a while to consider it a restorative tool. It is incredibly powerful because it requires a lot of you and your honesty, you and your love, you and your energy, you and your power. By being more mindful, living more intentionally, and becoming more aware of who I am and how I process pain, God has shown me how my art can be used as my form of ministry. When I photograph Black women, I want them to see themselves the way God sees them: beautiful, whole, magnificent, wonderfully made. Through my photography, I am able to reclaim my power. Beyond the beautiful photos, the intimate experiences that I get to create with other Black women are a love language. In being supportive of these women I am also supported, because there's a shared understanding that the woman facing me is a reflection of me and I am a reflection of her.

Resilience is about refusing to let my trauma make me small and always deciding to wake up every day to expand and take up space unapologetically. I'm not going to let anything make me feel unimportant. I latched on to a belief that I had no power for too long; but I do have my power. I do have a voice. Considering all the ways in which I've allowed my experiences to make me small, when I stand my ground and choose to self-advocate, it says, *Deun, you're powerful and you're important and you matter. By all means, you are worthy.*

Resilience is about refusing to let my trauma make me small and always deciding to wake up every day to expand and take up space unapologetically.

Raising My Inner Child Without Fear

Morgan Ashley
Cofounder, The Bohemian Brands

I was born in Berkeley and raised in Oakland. Oakland was all I knew growing up and has made me who I am. My pride for my city runs so deep, but as the Bay Area has begun to shift, it's also been increasingly centered on gentrification. I started college in San Francisco, but in 2008 when the economy fell, my school closed. Meanwhile, Proposition 8, a California ballot that opposed same-sex marriage, was passed as a state amendment. Watching people in my city protest gay marriage was shocking. As a queer woman, I grew up going to Pride every year, but watching the protests made me feel lost in my own home. If I was ever going to leave and move away, I knew then was the time.

I'd only visited Atlanta once before but had heard so many stories from Black folks who would return from their travels full of joyous moments centered around our culture. I applied for school in Atlanta, saved a few dollars, and bought a one-way ticket. When I told my mother that I'd made the decision to move to Atlanta, she cleaned out her savings account and handed me everything. Like Oakland, Atlanta felt comforting to me. It was beautiful to see the diversity of Black folks, but there was still an immense culture shock. People found

/trīb/

me different because of my West Coast accent and my vernacular. When I landed in 2009, I didn't have a single friend. I was out of my comfort zone with no safety net. It was hard for me to be away from everything I knew, but I believe you aren't really learning unless you're uncomfortable. I used to say that I wouldn't leave Atlanta until I conquered the city. Now, I don't believe any city can be conquered but instead think of it in terms of how to make myself a home and a community. By doing just that, I've matured here in Atlanta.

I've now settled into adulthood. Most people today describe me as a loudmouth, sometimes a confrontational, happy, and optimistic person, but I used to be a quiet, timid child. I had a hard time holding on to my boundaries, and I had bad social anxiety. Growing up, finding my own voice was challenging. When I was young, I was molested and almost kidnapped. Those experiences became a turning point for me. Those traumatic moments forced me to stand up for myself. I didn't want my story to be about pain and trauma. I didn't want to be a victim anymore. Going through that process, what I held on to the most are those people who supported me and really saw me through that pain. My mother, my family, my friends, and all of the Black women in my circle inspired me to break out of my shell. They are my landmarks that confirm who I am meant to be. Now, my inner child is awake and has the voice to speak up for herself, so that's what I'm doing. I am a loudmouth with a purpose. who knows who the fuck she is!

I am capable of tackling what life throws at me. In moments of uncertainty, I think about the phrase "Fear is a liar." It will have us doing things we shouldn't be or triggering our weaknesses. We all have insecurities, and it's important for us to have a mirror persona so that we're able to converse with ourselves. A year ago, I was depressed and living life unhappily. I didn't have the strength to motivate myself. I told my boss that I didn't want to be here. Alarmed, she set me up with a life coach. During that time, I also met with a therapist because I was not okay; I was dealing with thoughts of suicide. I had to say to my community, "I need help." I've learned in my adulthood that it's important to call on help and to tap into the beautiful resources available to many of us.

It takes a village to raise a child. My inner child and I need a whole damn village, as we all do. I want to be part of that village for other Black people, specifically Black women. The story I want to pass on is that I fiercely stand up for my people. My sense of pride in my roots and my Blackness is what makes me who I am. I love everything about what it means to be Black and a woman, even in this ridiculously racist country. My dedication to Black folks resonates in the work I do to celebrate Black creatives and brands, the words I speak, and the way I show up to illuminate our strengths. No matter what zip code I'm in, I will always ride for us!

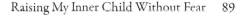

Butterflies Sat Next to My Heart

Dydine Umunyana

Human Rights Advocate and Author

Rwanda is my country of birth. That's where my story begins and where it always returns. My memories of Rwanda are painted with thoughts of a very community-oriented country, a place of a thousand hills and smiles, but also the pain behind those smiles. Within one hundred days, more than 800,000 lives were lost to the genocide against the Tutsis, and our country went through deep grief that consumed us. Every-one I grew up with and knew had lost something or someone; the country as a whole was mourning.

I was almost four years old when the genocide unfolded in Rwanda in 1994. My parents were young and were recruited to join the Uganda-based Rwanda Patriotic Front, the Tutsi-led political and military movement that ultimately ended the genocide and regained control of the country. My parents left my baby brother and me to be raised by our grandparents. Before 1994, we were a functional family, but the genocide changed everything. My grandmother had twelve children, and she lost six of them, and so it was with so many people that she grew up with.

The pain was too much for her to bear, and she fell into a deep depression. Her surviving children would need to remind her that they were still alive. I was so young at the time that my memories of the genocide itself are faint. Though to experience trauma, it's often enough to just feel the impact of tragedy on our community and our families. All I had to make sense of it all were nightmares in my dreams or pieces of stories I heard from family members and friends, which left me without a full understanding of what my family went through or how deeply they were traumatized. My grandmother wasn't ready to tell her story. Today I understand that we have to go through a lot of grieving and healing to be able to even see and share our own stories.

Both of my parents survived the genocide, but when they returned, they learned that their friends, families, and siblings had been killed. And like so many other people who felt alone and raw in the world post-genocide, neither of my parents had much to offer to console us because they were coping with loss in their own ways. My father couldn't see life after genocide. I had to learn about him and his experience through other people because he wasn't in a healthy mental space to be able to share his own story. Everything I heard from him was from a place of pain, and he would have frequent episodes of mental breakdowns. My parents' marriage crumbled soon after their return. My mother coped by being strong and sacrificing her emotions to take care of my siblings and me, not giving herself the time to grieve over the loss of her own siblings. It wasn't until recently that she started therapy for the first time and allowed herself to cry and react to what happened twenty-seven years ago. When I was writing my first book about the genocide, *Embracing Survival*, I did my research on my mother. I asked her tough questions about what she went through, and she was finally able to share some of her experiences, which has brought me a lot of closure as well.

Growing up, I didn't realize there was life outside of those stories of pain. I just thought life was that way, and it created overwhelming anger in me when I was a teenager. I was angry at everything and everyone, resentful that I was stuck in a world full of darkness. Instead of sharing it or learning how to deal with my anger, I shut down. As a teenager, I didn't quite understand the history of the country. But the more I learned about it, the more I was able to put things into perspective. While my family did struggle, it was nothing compared to what my friends and so many other Rwandans were going through and the losses they endured.

In high school I went to the Kigali Genocide Memorial for the first time. I learned about the divisiveness of ethnic groups and the roots of the genocide. Inside the memorial there is a room with large, beautiful photos of children on the walls with descriptions of who they were and the dreams that died with them. It was in that moment of standing in that room that I woke up to appreciate how lucky I was to just be alive. The odds had been against me, that I would lose my life in 1994, but I didn't. I made a decision then and there to not be a victim of my country's history but to use my life to help others also heal their trauma and embrace the blessing of life, shifting from blame to possibility.

Learning history is extremely therapeutic for the younger generations because it provides context our families cannot.

Twenty-seven years later, the genocide still affects both young and old generations deeply. It's still fairly recent and for many, even for those who were born after the genocide, the trauma is a firsthand experience. Their families experienced it and still haven't healed, and their trauma is passed down through each generation when not properly dealt with and healed. Learning history is extremely therapeutic for the younger generations because it provides context our families cannot. Between my brother Arstide Kanamugire and I, who were born right before the genocide, and my two younger siblings, Basil Boris Kanyamibwe and Betina Raissa Giramata, who were born after the genocide, there is a huge difference in the way we see life. My brother Arstide and I, and others who lived through the genocide, have vivid memories cemented in our minds and hearts and an instinctual awareness of the historical relationship between the Tutsis and Hutus. We've lost the matriarchs and patriarchs of our families who protected us, forcing us to learn to survive without them. The younger generation doesn't have those references, which allows them to have a freer spirit and have permission to feel and express themselves. In a way, the younger generation is healing the country's collective heartbreak.

Healing for me is a journey—an endless journey. It's my journey to not ignore my feelings and acknowledge what I went through while also recognizing how they have deeply influenced my decisions. Sharing and learning about other people's pain and how they have overcome has really helped me gain perspective. It gives me a sense of hope that I will get through whatever it is that I go through and reminds me that I'm not alone. Healing is a journey of telling myself that I'm going to be okay. We're all trying to find ourselves and to find our place in the world. We don't get to choose where we are born or the color of our skin or our ethnicities; these concepts may be hard to understand for some, especially children who may be wondering why we aren't handed the life we want. My hope is for others walking the world to know that they belong here in it, and that leading with love first—not hate—is how we'll all heal together.

The Current
of Adieu

I've mourned the loss of people who have passed and those still living, disappointed in their endings, frustrated that there was nowhere to channel the loss except in stillness and in time. Restlessness can make us unsure of how or where to package and place the memories we hold or had hoped to one day make. There are different currents to goodbyes. You can long for someone and still choose to let go, glad to wash them away. Your time together can end too soon, like an abrupt interruption to love. How do you find solace in releasing attachments that were once pillars in your genesis?

Unhealed Wounds

Chloe Dulce Louvouezo

His name was Guy*. You could call it love but it was codependency and control masquerading as love. My naivete paid the price. He was sixteen years my senior, with a physique that commanded and a gaze that wouldn't let loose. We met at a Howard homecoming, amid the rhythmic waves of dancing to blaring reggaeton beats. I fell in infatuation with Guy because he was everything I was not—assured, with a presence that either repelled you or lured you in and made you want to be on his team. For me it was the latter.

His eyes and scars told stories, and I was intrigued by them. He had anecdotes for every street corner in the city. His past was entangled with tales of money, drugs, violence, and prison. Riding alongside him as we drove through DC, I'd sit and listen to his accounts of a life of crime and punishment, looking out the window at the battered world that was once his. He was a changed man, he swore. It resonated, and I was impressionable. I understood what it meant to want to disentangle yourself from your past to reinvent a new narrative because I wanted the same. I was attracted to our differences and inspired by the idea that we could heal each other's wounds. In many ways, we were growing up together.

We quickly became interwoven into each other's lives. I was eager to love, and his attention convinced me I was getting it in return. Fresh out of college, the relationship thrust me into adulthood before I had a chance to know who I was and what I deserved. He soon became my chosen family—a father figure, best friend, and a lover in one, who filled voids I unknowingly had. The more I invested, the more I hoped for a reward that the relationship couldn't actually provide because he had wounds of his own that toxified us before we even rooted.

Though we came from different paths, Guy and I both knew what it was like to feel like outliers—the silver lining of our relationship that kept me anchored to him. But as much as I first believed our broken pieces could complete each other, I realized too late that the role he played in my life to fill the unresolved void of a father was not a saving grace. It was the gateway that gave him access to exploit my insecurities. His own essence was dimming, and he was feeding off my youth. The power dynamics soon shifted. His temper escalated with each passing argument, and my voice quieted. His looks of disapproval silenced me as the months and years passed, only further enticing me to want to love him better, deeper, and with everything I had to prove to both of us that I was a good partner. Until I had nothing left for myself and until he leveraged that against me. Cyclical apologies and promises got comfortable in our home—a

*His name has been changed.

response to the violence that normalized in his words and performance. It started with hurling objects across rooms, divisive attempts to isolate me from those I loved, and gaslighting that eroded my reality to convenience his disloyalty.

But all things on paper suggested we were building something. We bought a home together, a notable milestone for the both of us. The day after closing on the sale, I felt collected and accomplished. I was twenty-three years old with a deed. But my high sobered that night during a car ride home. A heated debate over lies and integrity led to a blackout and a bruised face. I woke up to my throbbing chin the size of a tennis ball as he parked the car in the driveway. Inside, I immediately showered, trying to scrub away the indignity. I sobbed silently under the steaming water as he banged on the door. My body stiffened with every jolting thump. After my shower, I sat on the couch next to him as he drowned out my physical pain with regrets and guarantees of more-loving tomorrows. I became emotionally numb as he pleaded for forgiveness. We were scheduled to move into our new home the next day. I felt cornered into accepting his assurances. The desire to be wanted compromised my strength in a moment when it was most needed. I ended the night surrendering my body to him, in the heat of his passionate professing of love. Similar nights ensued, yet I stayed, convinced that this was love, flawed but real. In the five years that followed, every bruise he left chipped at my self-trust and discernment to walk away. Not everyone in our lives is on divine assignment, I soon learned. Some people come to slay your spirit.

There was the time he punched my legs on the stairs, leaving my thighs shades of black and purple. The time he shoved his way into my friend's apartment and dragged me off her bed by my feet and down the hallway. The time I locked myself in the bathroom as he pounded it open, fearing that his wrath would leave me with the same beating he'd boasted having given his exes. The affairs with women whom he had me befriend and allowed to make themselves comfortable in our home and an ally in his deception. And the one that led to a secret child conceived and born, and the humiliation that followed as I tried to unravel myself from my life with him. What kept me from leaving was that I was looking to the person who wounded me to also heal me. Our dramas and my traumas became my dusty secret. I was too embarrassed to answer questions that would suggest my weaknesses. People ask women why they stay, wondering why we choose to compromise ourselves, their flustered eyebrows and tilted heads casting shadows of shame. Unknowingly, their questions scratch at the wounds we're still working to heal.

> The desire to be wanted compromised my strength in a moment when it was most needed.

I stayed because I was afraid of what I would be or not be without him. I stayed because I was tired of the revolving door of people and places that were passersby in my life. I wanted to plant my feet, and in pursuit of home, I was willing to sacrifice sanity and safety for a broken interpretation of security. I stayed because I didn't understand how to qualify and recognize authentic love and partnership. I didn't know myself well enough to trust that I knew what was best for me . . . so I let him lead. It was impossible to follow an example of love that I had never seen. The parallels between him and my father enabled undeserving tolerance. I stayed because I felt responsible for him. I believed I could love him all the way into being a better man. I cared to my own detriment and worried that no one would understand his wounds as much as I did. My unhinged loyalty held on to the blind faith that we were on a journey together and that we would both be better for it. I stayed because my courage to leave was overshadowed by his convincing conviction that through loyalty, I could redeem myself of the flaws he saw in me. The intensity we shared concealed the inequities in our relationship and, being young and hopeful, I mistook hook and reel for love.

After finally gathering enough pieces of myself to have the courage to leave, I found out I was pregnant. The circumstance could not have felt more disgraceful. He persisted in trying to lure me back home to rekindle our relationship, but with all certainty I decided to terminate the pregnancy. The least I could do, he said, was to let him be present for the procedure. The four-hour wait at the clinic felt endless. As I waited for my name to be called, sitting among the group of other women awaiting their turn with looks of angst sweeping their spirit, he pleaded for me to keep the pregnancy, swearing he was painfully aware of his flaws and deserving of redemption. For four hours he called on me to not go forward, to spare any last chance we had together by sparing the pregnancy. I was called to the back room alone and lay on the table in guilt and regret. Tears dripped down the sides of my cheeks as the twilight anesthesia gradually muted my cries.

When the procedure was over, two nurses walked me back to the waiting room, one of my arms draped over each of their shoulders. Our seats were empty; Guy had left. The toes of my shoes dragged on the dusty gravel as the nurses carried me outside, where he sat in the dark in his car. He barely lifted a finger as they positioned me in the front seat and closed the door behind me. For the next thirty minutes of the ride home, he berated me with slurs and vulgarity. He filled the car with words that disparaged, desperate to assign blame for not keeping the pregnancy because it was easier than accepting that I didn't want to water another one of his rotten seeds. He no longer had me hooked, and his lack of control and supremacy over me left him unhinged. But the anesthesia crippled me, and I didn't have the strength or consciousness to refute. I reclined my seat and stared at the passing trees as his shouting rang echoes in the car and drowned out the radio. He returned me home in pieces—heart and body shattered.

It took me years to recover from that day and that relationship. The entanglement of codependency and abuse created a compromising relationship with myself. The trauma I carried with me from it lay dormant until more of my whole self was needed to nurture the prospect of new budding relationships and

> I needed to see past the parts of my story that I wasn't proud of in order to make amends with the young woman that environment fostered.

friendships. I hadn't recognized it as trauma until escapism and distrust became patterns that distracted me from sitting deeply with the impact the shame had on my esteem. I needed to name my trauma and bring meaning to it in order to recognize my own self-worth. I needed to see past the parts of my story that I wasn't proud of in order to make amends with the young woman that environment fostered. I needed to forgive myself for being a product of my insecurities and of the longing for love I once had. I needed to wrap myself around she who was once shattered, until my own warmth mended my wounds.

New Beginnings

Adriana Parrish
Intuitive Medium Healer

I was born soon after my mom's high school graduation. Despite being very young, I can remember a tireless work ethic, a permanent task of goal setting, and her striving to achieve aims without ever sacrificing being such an amazing mother. Through new careers, she flourished, returning to school alongside a successful climb up the Department of Corrections, where she operated as an acting warden at one point. At work she was intense, resolute, and in command, but at home we saw a gentler side where she was the ultimate caretaker: sensitive, a good listener, and dedicated to every hat she wore.

Mom was a Mexican woman, born and raised in California, pregnant by a Black man, at a time that had yet to accept her decision socially. It was a big deal for my family, as she was the first to explore an interracial relationship that would birth children outside of her race. (My father's side of the family understood, through experience, how to live with diversity.)

Faced with struggles at home, my mother realized the challenges that lay ahead. She faced the struggle of my grandmother kicking her out while she was pregnant with me and no longer offering financial support for her. My grandmother wasn't accepting of their relationship either, but once I was born, she became able to move beyond it. We now share a very deep and meaningful connection, especially when it comes to our intuitive dreams. We both share the gift of having intuitive dreams before someone in the family falls ill or passes away. My grandmother has recently opened up and shared about our family lineage as healers in villages in Mexico.

I had a very traditional Mexican upbringing, yet my mother was also sensitive to my identity as a Black woman, tremendously ensuring culture existed on both sides for my three sisters and me. Awareness of our identity inspired confidence in a world not yet designed for mixed-raced children. Growing up as a mixed-race child, it was rare to identify with anyone. I didn't have the experience of friends with families that looked similar to mine, or with hair like mine. Still, it was challenging growing up biracial in a mostly white community that was also unaccepting of my mixed ethnicity.

My mother died in a car accident in January 2018, after leaving a doctor's appointment. It was the first rain of the season, so the roads were slippery. A five-car collision ensued, and she lost control of her vehicle and found herself in the direction of oncoming traffic where she hit a truck head-on.

Everyone else walked away from the accident. My mother was the only fatality. Life stopped when I got that phone call. I struggled

with how this could have happened and why. I felt lost, angry, and so traumatized that the reality of my mother's death didn't resonate with me. Instead, it was a bad movie. I remember seeing my mother's name in the newspapers written as "the deceased," and it felt unreal.

There wasn't any time for grieving. Naturally, I assumed the maternal role, as my mother was the matriarch of our family, and I was the firstborn, so I decided to display that strength and support for my sisters. As I recalled memories of her, my mother imparted her resilience onto me like an ancestral rite of passage. And that fortitude flows down our lineage to my sisters, cousins, tía, even my grandmother. It's our connection to this strength that keeps me fighting each day after her passing. Between her funeral, organizing fiscal responsibilities, and dealing with the accident's legal aftermath and her house, I felt the weight of two worlds on my shoulders. Thoughts of the sort of strength my mother would act out during a challenging time like this continuously played in my mind. I witnessed my mother act out this strength when she lost her father at the age of thirty-one and was pregnant with my youngest sister.

My daughter Siena was just four months old when Mom died. I was barely adjusting to motherhood. But when Siena was born, my

mom came up to Oakland to help me as a new parent. I was nervous about maternity, but she gave me the determination to handle it.

Our mother-daughter friendship taught me how to have the same relationship with my daughter. My mother and I joked around and said that we grew up together because she had me so young and was still growing into the woman she wanted to become.

Looking back, I learned the value of a family bond and celebrating life from her. As a mother myself, her passing puts more importance on spending time with my daughter so that I can support her as a mother and friend just as my own did.

I have conversations with my daughter about her grandmother. It keeps the memories of her alive to awaken the many stories and

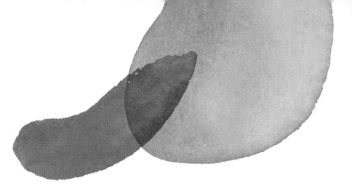

photos we have of her. My mother is very much present in our home, and even though she's not here physically, she is very much a part of my daughter's life.

Since those early months after her passing, I have allowed myself the space to feel and sit with my emotions—whatever they are—without feeling pressured to deal with them any particular way. Some days I'm full of gratitude. Other days I write her letters as though she were still here and share things with her or cry if I need to, and it keeps me tethered to my mother's voice.

I know she would be proud of me. I've grown much through my experiences as a woman, mother, wife, and sister, allowing me to open up and get more comfortable with emotions than ever before. Even now, she is leading me to my healing work.

For as long as I can remember, I had visions of my late grandfather. Every time he would leave, I would wake up crying because it felt otherworldly yet still real. I would share these dreams with my mother over the years, and she always welcomed them without judgment. Growing up Catholic, it was incredibly taboo to have visions, but I became very comfortable with them because they were frequent.

After my mother passed away, she started speaking to me in the same manner through my dreams. It brought me peace because we all have our day to go, and there's nothing we can do to change that. When it's your time to go, it's your time to go. No matter where you are, where you're going, what's happening in your life, or how much you love someone.

In these dreams, she was telling me to keep listening and follow my intuition as I moved forward. I have always been leery of medium readings, but after my mother's passing, I decided to connect with a Berkeley spiritualist. Without offering any context, she immediately recounted direct messages from my mother and details about the accident. My dreams began getting stronger after that, and I can't help but think it was my mother steering me toward the healing work I now perform in grief trauma/therapy by aiding people to begin their journey to healing. I do this as a medium by bringing forward messages from loved ones who have passed away in order for people to begin healing from their loss.

Communication with ancestors takes us to another vibration by allowing open connections beyond the physical. When we can get to that space energetically in our meditation and breath work, it's enlightening. This level of understanding opened a new realm for me. Before this insight, I hadn't paid much attention to my gift in any way. I was going through

UNTIL ONE DEALS WITH SORROW, YOU DON'T HAVE A FRAME OF REFERENCE FOR PROCESSING IT.

the motions of life without having any presence of mind. Until one deals with sorrow, you don't have a frame of reference for processing it.

Never in a million years would I have thought that intuitive/mediumship work would create a life change for me, and because of it, I am mindfully walking down a new road. It's made me question everything I was sure about before, including my faith (which I lean into even more than before).

I'm scratching the surface of this ability, but it arises in you when you're open to receiving a greater peace. I've endured much loss in the past few years. Yet, I feel a lot more connected to my mom than ever before, which I know may read strange for some, but it's a newfound intimacy we share.

There is a summoning at work, a call to aid others in their healing journey, recognizing that grief and loss look different for everyone. I want to help people understand that the ending of something is not the ending of everything. Even in challenging moments of loss, there's more life ahead.

I want people to know that some things have to come to an end to reap new beginnings.

Her Cracked-Open Heart Is Never in Vain

Orixa Jones
Founder, Bad Girl, Good Human

A few years ago, I was in a really low place. I was trying to figure out where I was going and what I wanted to do with my life. I dabbled in blogging and photography, but it wasn't really working out for me. I felt discouraged and couldn't see past what I thought was failure. I struggled financially, but since it was the first time I had stepped out on my own away from my family, I refused to go home. It would feel like a step back, and I didn't want to lose any momentum in my exploration. I didn't want to lose any momentum in my exploration. I had to shove my pride aside and figure it out. For eight months, I couch-surfed with no home of my own while trying to grow my business, Bad Girl, Good Human. The hardest part of the process of getting it off the ground was not letting my ego get in the way. I've always had a hard time asking for help because I associated it with weakness when I was younger. But starting something with so much ambiguity required me to sacrifice pride for possibility by asking for help. It required me to be grounded in humility. During that time, I was able to build something out of nothing. Those were some of the toughest months of my life because they stretched me to prove to myself what I was made of. Now, I'm not too proud to fail. There is something to be gained from every fall, every tumble. It helps me move more quickly through figuring out what does and doesn't work, and makes the failure not so painful.

Since then, both my business and I have grown tremendously. I've been able to really fall into my work hard and heavy. Through the community I've curated with Bad Girl, Good Human, I want to offer other women something I never had: a blank canvas for them to explore their own spectrum of being multidimensional. I didn't have permission to do that myself when I was younger, which caused mental and emotional turmoil in my life. My mother had passed down her own traumas to me—traumas I wasn't even aware of. I was raised in an environment where I wasn't allowed to react and respond; to be expressive was considered disrespectful. I've always had this sense of duality, but in my teenage years, I didn't have the language to articulate or accept all of me because I was taught to suppress my feelings. I was curious, and, as relationships started to form and with experience, I began to embrace the many sides of myself that my childhood didn't have the chance to explore. Today I recognize the different women that make up me. I think of myself as a bad girl, good human.

They're both traumatic, but because heartbreak is still alive and feels tangible, it's easier to mourn that than it is to grieve death.

I recognize the woman that is the caregiver. I recognize the woman that is resilient. I recognize the woman that is very soft and meek. I recognize the woman that you don't want to fuck with. And I also recognize the woman I aspire to be. Creating a safe space for women to just be invites them to be themselves, cry if they need to, rebuild, and get back into the world when they feel like they can bear it. If I had had access to the space that I'm creating now for other women when I was younger, I would have had deeper self-awareness of the spectrum of my feelings that I've never been able to name.

Bad girl, good human is how I live my life, and represents the duality of who I am and the ebbs and flows of my life experiences. There is no up without a down and vice versa. There is no positive without a negative. There is no success without failure. One can't happen without the other. It's called balance. And while I've had some successes, I can't say that I'm truly at peace with my past struggles. I am navigating them more gracefully and with more poise, but the work is not done, and I don't think it will ever be done.

I'm learning this through both my professional and personal life. There are times in heartbreak or loss when I don't feel like I can repair myself, and that's when the work is needed the most. I'm full of scars and scrapes and holes and bruises. This year I lost my brother to cancer, and it's been the craziest whirlwind of emotions. I watched him die within months. We found out on Christmas Eve, and he went in March. My therapist asked me if it is easier to mourn romantic heartbreak than it is to mourn the loss of my brother. They're both traumatic, but because heartbreak is still alive and feels tangible, it's easier to mourn that than it is to grieve death. I'm still blown away by that question, and I don't know if I can answer it yet.

Seeing his death firsthand and up close did something to me. It has made me more time-sensitive and made me want to extend the olive branch to the people I love most with the time I have left on earth. When it comes to matters of the heart, I'm now sensitive about making the relationships with the people who are still living count. Feelings are such a complex thing. I'm learning to work through very raw emotions of grief in loss—in loss of all kinds. There's fruitful loss, and there's loss you mourn. I give myself grace by allowing myself to feel whatever I'm going to feel for however long it lasts. Only then will I be able to move through it. Though time can feel like it's crawling, having the comparison of death makes our living so much more real and time bound.

My Father's Smell

Offeibea Obubah
Global Health Strategist

My father's name is Ernest "Beena" Obubah. He was vivacious and an immaculate dresser. He loved his wife, was proud of his son, and cherished his daughter. He loved scotch neat, and he loved people. He had flaws, but I can't trace those in photographs. From the few pictures my mother did not destroy, I gathered that my father was tall and lean and handsome with the kind of beauty that appealed to only a few. So many parts of him still come to life on my face. My reddish-pink lower lip hangs low just like his. My lean fingers are his. My smile is his.

He died when I was two years old in 1989, and for a little over five years, not a single family member revealed this secret to me. There were myriad stories about his whereabouts. The stories went like this: "*Maama, wo papa kɔ sea*" (Maama, your dad is gone to sea) or "*Maama, wo papa kɔ abrokyire*" (Maama, your dad is in the west), sometimes in Akuapem but most often in Fante, the two native Ghanaian languages spoken in our home. For years my paternal grandmother would visit my brother and me from Sekyikrom, Ghana, my father's birthplace. She always came bearing gifts, "From your father," she would say.

My denial of my father's death started in 1994, when I was seven years old and finally learned the truth about his passing. It was on the fifth anniversary of his death. Family and family friends all gathered at a church, but I hadn't made the connection and didn't realize we were attending his memorial until an aunt accidentally said, "Oh, your dad would have been so proud of you if he was alive."

I froze. I couldn't process what she'd said and the reality that he was really gone. I asked my mother and brother in the car on the way home if what the woman had said was truth—and they confirmed it. My heart sunk.

I was livid, and I felt robbed of this feeling of having a father who was alive but far. Then I turned to denial, a denial that consumed me for years because this loss had now been cemented as part of my family's story. I cannot tell you the exact moment I released this denial, yet at some point, it left me. But then I became engulfed with grief, which I am still working through today. Some days it's subtle, other days I cry without warning even to myself. This sort of grief, it lies low then it rises like the ocean waves that make you tumble. Grief for a parent is difficult even for the children who missed the genesis of the collective grief. Finding out about my father's death years later didn't mean it hurt any less. The reality that I've never been able to call upon him for anything—neither in my childhood nor in my adulthood, when I desperately needed dating advice—makes me wonder what name I would have called him by in times of need.

*Daaa, in my toddler years when I needed his
attention.*
*Dad, in my teenage years while I straddled
between holding on to him and letting
him go.*
*Daddy, in his later years to remind him that I
was still his little girl.*
*Papa, definitely maybe Papa. I would have
wanted a name for him that was just
between the two of us that no one—not
even my brother—could share.*

My older brother, my wonderful brother, became both my brother and my father at a young age. I still do not know how he processed the death of the father he knew in the flesh. He never speaks of it, so I speak for us both.

It's a hollow feeling.
It sinks deep within you and is unreachable.
*You cannot fill it with any other love, not even
that of the living parent.*
*So, we walk around half empty in search of a
thing, anything to fill this gap.*
*Sometimes we are a burden on our loved ones
because we require too much love from them.*

My mother has never told my brother or me where our father is buried. I suppose she's still processing her grief for the man who vowed to never leave her but left and never came back.

I wish I knew where he lies. I would like to go and sit at the feet of his burial site and feast with him, whatever way the dead and the living can break bread together. I want to tell him that I am his daughter and that I miss him immensely, but I am sure he knows that already.

I search for my father in men and in places where he has never been. But there are always reminders that he never left, and his spirit still wanders in my life.

*I walked into an elevator and a man smelled like
something I presumed my father would have
smelled like, so I closed my eyes and inhaled
deeper to fill my lungs, and then I smiled.*
Well, there was no man in the elevator.
But I think there must have been a man.
There definitely was a man.
*Because there it was…what my father's smell
could have been.*

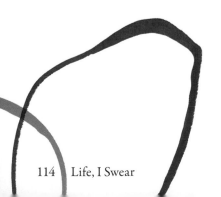

I SEARCH FOR
MY FATHER IN MEN
AND IN PLACES
WHERE HE HAS
NEVER BEEN.

le calme me libre

PART III

PEACE IT
TOGETHER

If the Heart Could Talk

O ur greatest love stories are those centered on how we cultivate relationships with ourselves. If the heart could talk, mine would tell me to rest, child. She would remind me that our intake is more important than our output, and knowing the distinction allows us to set boundaries that make replenishing possible. Our value is not in what we do for others; it is in who we inherently are. Rest has become forcign to our overworked hearts, but when we're still enough to listen to the whispers of our needs, we're able to honor the love we both give and require.

Love After Love

Chloe Dulce Louvouezo

I learned love from fragmented sources entangled in secrets, lust, and self-doubt. Examples of what I assumed was love instead modeled selfless sacrifices that rarely saw their return. There was little to inspire my imitation of love but the naive hope that I could manifest a right relationship with the wrong partner. I went through the motions with a muddled understanding of what I was losing by being too flexible and too submissive to the hope of being loved back. My relationships were not reciprocal. They distracted me from trusting myself and thus from loving wisely.

After my relationship with Guy and a few years of anticlimactic dating, I fell into a romance with my next future ex. The start of it felt well placed, like we just made sense. In many ways, his background as a cultural nomad and an inquisitive creative mirrored mine, and we navigated our experiences together with ease and comfort. He related to diasporic identity and if for that alone, I saw a home in him. He was a charmer and a conversationalist with a warm and inviting energy. But the relationship wasn't deeply seated, and I was soon blindsided by what I did not know of him. I hadn't asked

I hadn't demanded the truth and transparency that the foundation of love deserves.

the right questions. Jamila Woods's "Sonia" song now chimes on repeat when I think about what those should have been. "What's your ideology? Do you love yourself? Are you healing your trauma? What's your concept of wealth? Do you love your mama?" I hadn't demanded the truth and transparency that the foundation of love deserves. The answers to those questions, had they been asked, would have revealed just how much we were not in harmony.

Our relationship centered on blind spots I didn't know existed. I enabled his irresponsibility and gambling compulsions unknowingly at first, and later through denial. Somewhere along the way, I recognized that there was a purity that was missing from the basis of our love, yet as two dreamers, we carried on with audacious plans together. We started a family, had a wedding, and both continued to hope that the underpinning of our love would come after we settled into our life together. But it didn't work that way (it never does), and soon we lost our warmth and our promise. Very shortly after our wedding, our union became unsavory.

After learning the hard way, now I know that trust should be earned in droplets and lost in buckets. What I did not know before was that I was in a relationship with someone who didn't have the capacity to live in authenticity and confidence. His chasing of brittle and fickle dreams distracted him from being present. He was out of touch with his alignment, and his own impulses to chase those dreams overtook his ability to nurture his family the way I hoped. The carelessness of his decisions disrupted my peace. Despite always having had the spirit of a wanderlust, being thrust into the chaos made me yearn for the predictability of stability. I was pregnant with our second son, living in hesitation, and tiptoeing around the fragilities of the landmine that had become our life. I woke up one payday to two overdrawn bank accounts. I thought about how much more staying would cost me if I did not walk away.

Leaving that relationship felt gutsy. Opting for single motherhood over partnership while expecting was bold but necessary. I was terrified of the journey ahead, but more than

The gentler I was with myself through the language I used and the margin of error I allowed, the more I humanized myself.

that, I knew I deserved peace. I was ready to surrender to the pull from God that was telling me I had so much more to both receive and learn from love. After cycles of pouring into unhealthy relationships, it became clear that if I wasn't intentional about working in better partnership with myself, that I would self-sabotage. For too long, I extended myself for others and neglected my own needs. Sacrificing my aspirations for those of partners left me in shortage of self-worth values, which became a revolving door of deficit-based thinking around what I was made or capable of. I had to make space for my personal restoration without being upset at the fading dream of partnership. The day I ended that relationship was the day I learned boundaries.

For the next year I centered my energy around radical self-love and honest intentionality. I needed time to learn self-trust. I had dwelled in my own self-doubt for too long, and it became damaging to carry those dead thoughts into new life. That year was spent unpacking my patterns of choosing grace for others over grace for myself, working through trauma that had tormented my health, and finding stability in stillness and in rest. The gentler I was with myself through the language I used and the margin of error I allowed, the more I humanized myself.

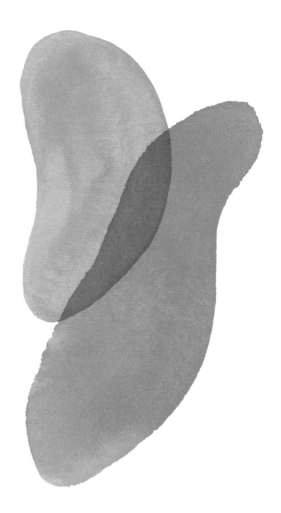

So, I regrouped with the many versions of myself from past and present to grant them all pardon—for not knowing or doing more than they had the capacity to at each juncture of their journeys. I let go, as much of the things I held against myself as I held against others. I released harbored resentment over endings of which I had no control; resentment that occupied energy it didn't deserve. I let every feeling—hurt, anger, and everything in between—run its course, then made joy a choice. In less mature chapters of my life, it would have been easier to allow tension to clog my spiritual pores than to try to understand my own role in my history's patterns. But if we're not decisive about boundaries that preserve our peace, we continue to be susceptible to unnec-

essary pain. The source of my peace came from studying and forgiving the experiences that robbed me of it. It came from rekindling flames in me that only I could ignite, if only I committed to relearning myself.

Starting years ago, when my spirit felt low, I would take a moment to stare at my reflection in the mirror as a way to pull myself together. I would get close up to study the texture of my hair, the curl of my eyelashes, and the pupils of my eyes long enough to discover new details of my imperfections I had never given attention to. In those moments, I let myself just be human, reminded by the very real senses of liquid salt tears from my eyes or the heat of my breath bouncing off the glass and back onto my lips. If only for a moment, I wanted to recognize myself. For a season, I had lost myself to reckless abandon of my own value. As the only intimacy I shared with myself amid being everything to everyone else, those minutes with the mirror were all I had. A decade later, I now return to the mirror. I look back at the woman before me. Aging laugh lines and growing freckles that I've never noticed stare back at me, and I realize how much time I've let pass without honoring those blemishes. I hadn't taken inventory of the life growing on my face. And I've needed a reintroduction to the intimacy I once shared with myself.

A Sacred Discovery

Alexandra Elle
Poet and Author

As someone who has struggled to find their way in the world, writing has really saved me. My journal has saved me. The pen and paper have saved me time and time again. To be an author of my life has shown me that I can stand in my power and that I can heal myself by anchoring onto self-trust. I want others to experience that same self-trust and that same anchoring in their writing practice and in their truth. I am honored that people trust me to stand beside them in their journey through writing, truth-telling, and self-care practice.

I want to gift people their own voice through writing. Having honest and open-ended conversations with our inner self and knowing that we can trust ourselves allow us to be our own greatest teacher. When we're able to find healing through the journey to joy—whether in silence or in sisterhood—we're better able to name our needs. As women, we're constantly holding others up. We're constantly taking care of home and showing up at work and being a friend and building our own communities and trying to keep it together. But sometimes we don't have space to keep ourselves together. Sometimes we really need to give ourselves permission to let go and to fall apart. In that falling apart, that's when we're really able to see what we need and how to ask for it. It doesn't have to be an intense moment of decision-making. It can be as simple as yes or no. It's about having the discernment of self-trust and knowing when to share and when not to. That requires us to get to know ourselves on deeper levels so that we can really experience what self-trust looks, feels, and tastes like and everything else in between. Everything starts with self.

I became a mother at the age of eighteen. It was not an ideal situation but something that shifted my identity for the better. Now, as a thirty-one-year-old woman, I can look back and know that I stood in my power by making the choice to change. Back then as a teenager, I didn't have the language to articulate my evolution. As I look back, I see that's when I was really creating a home for myself by deciding that I could change my life and I could also trust the trajectory in which I wanted my life to go. As an adult now with multiple children, with a husband, and a different sense of home, it has been pivotal to my healing process to do the work to become who I am. That in itself has created a home of love for those around me. I'm able to fill myself up in new ways and in turn, I can then offer that love to my family. That is really what makes a home: love. I am a home to self-love. The extension of the love that I offer and that I receive also makes me think of home, and what home should feel like.

When I can't write and need something to lean on, I tap into my spirituality, which is channeled by curiosity. I like the power of asking questions and searching for something that may never make sense. That's the beauty of being free to choose what you believe in. It's important for us to stay curious in whatever it is we're practicing and resting our faith in, because there is no finite answer in life. It is ever flowing and growing. What does God look like for you in your life and in your work? What does a higher spirit feel like? What does that energy move you to do? These questions all come down to curiosity. I am so intrigued by the spirit of a higher power and the spirit of divine alignment and how all of those energies speak to me and show up in my work.

I've also been called to find bravery in being curious about my shame, my guilt, my regrets, and my shortcomings, and greeting them all with questions. It's only right to be curious, to ask questions about how things have made us feel and what we've learned from them. Inner dialogue helps us get to the root of who we are and how we deal with those things. I still struggle with negative narratives of myself. After all, we're human. Even those of us who have found our path to healing and self-love still detour. We sometimes feel like we're not worthy or feel like we're not enough. And when that happens, I have to talk about it and lean on my community to love me through my hard times. It helps me return to writing to see my power and my truth and be reminded that I can move forward.

I find joy in the self-love that I practice, though I'm learning that joy will come and go. I used to chase joy. Chase it and then want to keep it forever. But that's not how life works. We have joyful moments, and we have painful moments. After we have those painful moments, after we're thrown for a loop in life, when joy shows up again, it's something special. We're born to know both joy and pain. That's what makes joy such a sacred discovery.

WE'RE BORN TO
KNOW BOTH JOY
AND PAIN. THAT'S
WHAT MAKES JOY
SUCH A SACRED
DISCOVERY.

Triumph of a Broken Heart

Kalkidan Gebreyohannes

Co-Founder, Black Girls, Green House

My love journey started at an early age. My relationship with my parents really informed how I wanted to be loved, how I loved other people, and what I thought love was. It propelled me on a journey of wanting to master love. As I got older and more experienced, I realized that it is an ongoing feat, and while we may forever try to master love, I don't know that we ever do. I genuinely value the idea of love, what it can provide me, and its healing power. And when you value something, you take care of it. You want to keep it, and you find ways to elevate it.

Love is something I've always wanted, that I've chased after ever since a young age. My love journey was complicated in a lot of ways, because I had expectations of things that I needed from a partner, but I hadn't quite understood how to first provide them to myself and for myself before expecting them from others. In college and after graduation, I was in a pretty significant relationship that ended really abruptly. My boyfriend's brother passed away, and it took a hard toll on him, which led to the end of our relationship. I left Detroit, where I was living at the time, and moved to Los Angeles with $237 to my name. Shortly after I relocated, I met my now ex-husband. He is an incredible person, and over the next thirteen years we had

three beautiful children. While we weren't meant to be married any longer, we were definitely meant to be family and to bring our children into this world together. We chose to keep our best-friendship intact. There was no grand betrayal or deceit. We understood where we were at. We understood some of the demons and things that we were fighting within our marriage, and that we had reached its end. We ended the relationship the same way we entered it, with peace and love. That was something that was important for me. So often we enter into relationships with so much excitement and zest and end them with so much anger and animosity, to the point where we wonder how we ever cared for or loved these persons to begin with. I think that's a true testament and challenge for ourselves to try to end things in love—for our own peace, health, and sanity.

When you believe that you're going to build something for a lifetime with someone, you hope that you get to commit to those words, promises, and covenants with each other always. The reality is that sometimes it doesn't work. We don't talk about heartbreak enough, and when we do it comes from a place of so much pain. I really challenge us to look at our heartbreak as liberating, as empowering, as lessons learned, and as a mold for a better self. Heartbreak is an opportunity to

Self-preserving—keeping parts of ourselves intact—guarantees that we'll always have something to build upon.

learn and to grow. It's an opportunity to own our role in the failures of our relationships. The grace comes in how we're able to speak to ourselves in a voice that says we're human and we're better for it. It's hard to see that silver lining in the moment of relationship separation, and it can be quite painful to mourn past partners. While I know heartbreaks really can feel like death, collectively I want us to start shifting to the idea of letting people go.

I consider relationships to be like train rides: some people stay on from the first to the last stop with you, some people will come on at the third stop and get off at the eighth stop. It's all ever-moving and changing. The more relationships we enter and end, it's easy to feel increasingly lost after each one. Over time, we get beaten down. We start to slowly lose hope or lose sight of what feels healthy, what feels good, what feels safe. We're often left with no foundation because we're giving all of ourselves away and needing to rebuild ourselves at the start of every new relationship. That's why it's so important to maintain parts of ourselves for ourselves. Self-preserving—keeping parts of ourselves intact—guarantees that we'll always have something to build upon. I haven't always been great at it. Sometimes I think that I have, but when a relationship goes south, I'll realize how much I gave.

Through relationships, I've learned so much about myself, as they have been a mirror reflection of the areas of life that I value and where I need to improve. Love requires you to show up in ways that are unraveling and raw. If you haven't met yourself, if you do not yet understand yourself, if you've not gone into a relationship being very clear about what you need and how you need it, it's really hard to expect it and to communicate it. Love is a responsibility. I've worked really hard on understanding my needs, and I challenge myself to hear as best as possible the needs of my partner, and to filter them through an open mind. That's my reciprocity. And when I understand and I know better, then I can do better and I can love harder.

Today, love for me feels like peace and joy. When my peace has been distracted, it's hard to get back on track. I value my peace and my joy and want to extend those things to the people I love. Our intuition is strong enough to tell us when either is feeling off-kilter. It feels like unrest and like there's a war happening internally in our spirit when peace and joy are missing. It's in quiet moments with ourselves that we're able to hear clearly how to move and where to invest our energy. I honor my isolation and make room to hear myself, but I also make room for companionship and fellowship. All of them can live within me.

Loving All the Pieces of My Heart

Esther Boykin
Marriage and Family Therapist

My life today is a reminder of all the pieces that have unraveled, that I've picked up and put back together. When you feel fragile and it feels like everything's coming apart, it's easy to focus on what's missing and forget how many pieces there used to be. I felt very suffocated toward the end of my marriage. I loved my ex-husband, but the rules of our dynamic left no room for me to be my whole self. So many of my passions and preferences were abandoned to make space for marriage and children that eventually I forgot how to make space for myself.

Tending to ourselves takes a lot of practice and mindful effort. As Black women, we find that hard to do. We are socialized and encouraged to take care of others ahead of ourselves, and to be all things to everyone, which means there's always something more to live up to. We're complimented for being superwomen, which implies that not only can we do anything but that we have no needs of our own. As wives and girlfriends, we often put our goals, ambitions, and even preferences aside to support partners. As mothers, we set aside our fears and

dreams to encourage, support, and protect our children. We compromise our dreams and our self-care to be on call for the needs of those we are meant to take care of.

The question I ask myself most often is *Am I doing enough?* There is this part of me that feels like I always need to do more no matter how much I do. I should be working harder, more diligently. I should be doing more of *something*. And when I'm not doing what I know I need to do, rather than being gentle and compassionate with myself, I scold myself. This has seeped into old relationship patterns of feeling like I've needed to prove myself. For so long I believed I was loved because of the way I showed up and took care of others rather than loved simply because of who I am and just being present in

the world. It took recognizing this pattern in adulthood, in particular in my marriage and romantic relationships, for me to see that it was an internal belief I had held in childhood as well. Despite my parents constantly telling me how loved and special I was, I saw how they worked hard and how important *doing* things were in their lives—doing for me, for my extended family, for their students, and for strangers. After their divorce I didn't trust love as a constant in life and unconsciously developed a belief that one has to work hard and achieve a lot in order to create emotional safety and have love that lasts. Since my marriage ended, I've been able to step back and give myself credit to believe that what I offer based on who I inherently am is more than enough. Just me is plenty.

One thing that has been most challenging is noticing and owning the things that are less ideal about myself. Anything less than the idealized "evolved" version of myself gets some internal criticism, from being insular and stoic at times to resisting vulnerability when I'm under stress or fearful. As a relationship therapist, I always hold myself to the highest standard of emotional maturity instead of giving myself grace to be human and simply show up as my best even on days when my best isn't very much. Whatever our shit is, we create patterns of negative internal stories. But we can't condemn the areas of ourselves that still need work—we need to come to terms with them to get to a place of having more compassion for ourselves. Too often, others don't let us be whole, messy, complicated, and human. Society, culture, family, and race relations in America come together to really say to Black women, "This is who you're supposed to be. This is how you have to be." If you're crying, you're hysterical. If you're angry, you're a bitch. You're doing too much. These messages force us to hold it all together and constantly hover in suffocating spaces. And for me, these external messages convinced me to hide my full, complicated self for too long. But that's not how humanity works. We live inside concentric circles of cultures—the family we grew up in, our relationships, the broader culture of our communities. From all of those places and contexts is often a message that it's not okay to be complicated—but people are complicated.

The relationships I've cultivated since my marriage have held a mirror to the things I have to work on. The experience of being in relationships with people who only want you to show up fully and be present, who are not expecting you to take care of them and over-function for them gives them the opportunity to truly see you. They're able to see parts of you that even you haven't noticed about yourself. Relationships drive us as humans because we all deeply care about our connections to other people. We can use relationships as a place to cultivate a skill. Self-compassion and vulnerability are skills we have to practice. Learning to challenge our inner critic and contemplate the less helpful narratives in our head is a skill. When we're able to apply these skills in relationships with other people and grant others grace, it becomes a model for how we should also treat ourselves. It's not always comfortable, but that level of vulnerability is the road that leads us to deeper emotional intimacy. Understanding this concept has allowed me to experience myself in new ways.

Too often, others don't let us be whole, messy, complicated, and human.

Kin and Kindred Spirits

Brooke Hall
Producer

Estrogen. Growing up, it was everywhere in our home. You couldn't hide from it. You couldn't run from it. You couldn't dilute it. You had to love it and embrace it. I'm the youngest of four girls. My three sisters are eleven to seventeen years older than me. Our home was exciting but full of chaos and all the drama you'd expect from a house full of women. My sisters were emotionally evolving, rebellious, and exploring their identities. As the youngest, I was on the sidelines of the action, watching them navigate life as an adolescent. Each of them had distinct personalities, which brought a host of experiences. I enjoyed their differences and the uniqueness they brought to my life. I loved witnessing and learning the complexities of womanhood as a child. I felt deeply cared for as the baby of the family, and I knew, without question, that I was loved in our home.

My eldest sister, Ronnette, gave birth to my first niece shortly before her high school graduation. I was only two years old. I don't remember her not being a mother, and she was always a maternal figure in my eyes. Loyal, nurturing, and a leader, she made sure these were attributes I attained. Even when we were quarreling with each other, Ronnette made sure that sisterhood was a bond among us all. Because we did not live in the most peaceful neighborhood, conflicts with other girls were a regular occurrence. Ronnette always displayed a fiery shield of unwavering protection. It was instinctive and could not be turned off.

I always considered Ronnette to be mentally and spiritually strong; however, my early memories of her include an abusive relationship and trials as a single mother. It was mind-blowing to try to comprehend what led her to those dynamics. As a child, I often wondered why she found love in toxicity when she experienced so much love at home. I empathized with her when she lost her resilience, but I also felt deeply impacted by the drama she experienced. This comes with the heart connection of sisterhood. Witnessing how ugly it got for her taught me exactly what I didn't want in relationships and how to recognize red flags that lead to abuse. However, through her, I also learned how to have grace for my sisters and others. When people fail themselves, they also fail others by default. It's not intentional, nor should they be ostracized. She has rebounded as a better, stronger woman and a secondary matriarch of our family. Through Ronnette, I've not only learned the power of reinventing yourself, but also how to recognize and leave undeserving relationships and situations without hesitation.

Rica, my second-oldest sister, taught me how to read, ride a bike, tie my shoes, and to be self-sufficient much earlier than most children. Rica has been physically paralyzed on her left side since she was five years old, long before I was born. I realized at an early age that she wasn't capable of doing everything. Even as a child, I had a deep sympathy and compassion for her. At times, I would experience her bouts of frustration when she was reminded of her limitations. These bouts were expressed in different ways: in moodiness, isolation, or long walks with just her venting. She has never been one to make excuses, as she takes pride in her independence. Rica would push me beyond my limits and believed I could achieve anything. I often feel as though she lives vicariously through me. Because of her, I feel obliged to explore the world on her behalf. Rica, who is a mother of two, showed me resilience, empathy, patience. The value she has added to my life is priceless.

Through my sisterhood at home, I learned unconditional love.

Ronica, who is the youngest of my three older sisters, was the popular girl at school. The high school cheerleader who dated the cool football player and was an all-around "cool kid," that was Ronica. As children, our relationship was tense. She tolerated me, but I never felt that she wanted to make space for me as the new baby. Coveted by everyone and the "new" apple of my father's eye, I disrupted her place in the family. I desperately wanted to earn her attention. I wanted her to like me. My early experience with her led to unusually high expectations of loyalty from my friends in my teenage years. Any need to seek approval and acceptance in friendships would send me flying in the opposite direction. But Ronica also taught me confidence. I watched her pursue everything in life with an air of excellence. That drives my own ambitions even today. Ronica's a teacher's teacher whose guidance and support led to many milestones in my life. Although we have opposite personalities and opposite love languages, we have become the best of friends and have developed the closest of bonds in our adult years.

Even among themselves, my sisters had little in common, and their social lives didn't integrate. Through my sisterhood at home, I learned unconditional love—my parents made it clear that despite our very distinct personalities and lifestyles, we would respect and sup-

port each other as long as we lived under their roof. My father made sure we understood our responsibility to care for each other in spite of our grievances. He made sure our sisterhood was built on strong principles. Our closeness was supported by default of us having to stick together. Of all the things we could do wrong, fighting or tearing each other down was never permitted and was always met with harsh punishment. We weren't allowed to disrespect nor dishonor each other, because we were each other's keepers. We valued integrity and honesty, which provided space for self-expression and open conversation between us. We spoke our minds—not always with tact—but in a way that didn't allow resentment to fester. There wasn't much to hide, and we generally always spoke out about how we felt without fear of retribution; there was little reason to be disingenuous.

I've also learned the importance of loving people you don't always share commonalities with. What made my sisters and I sustain our loyalty toward each other despite our very stark differences was our shared values and virtues from living under the same roof. In friendships, it's easy to gravitate to those who are just like you in surface-level interests, but I like to quickly get to the core of who women are at their essence, which for the most part can only be accessed when you get into the weeds. When you love

someone you may not have much in common with, you have to dive deeper to find the qualities that make loving them easier. Most everyone deserves that type of unwavering love.

Now that I'm an adult and no longer under my sisters' wings, I don't know how to draw the line between friend and sister. Sisterhood is what I know and prefer. It's very much a quality-over-quantity thing. I had to understand that people aren't obligated to love me just because I'm their sister. In a family, you can't dismiss your sisters just because of disagreements or misalignments or miscommunications. It's okay to have boundaries, but opting out of sisterhood is *not* an option. I bring that same loyalty into my friendship sisterhoods.

I also bring the gentleness of being the baby of the family, though that is something I

AS BLACK WOMEN,
WE HAVE NOT
BEEN AFFORDED
SOFTNESS FROM
OTHERS AND
THAT NEGATIVELY
AFFECTS OUR
INTIMACY WITH
ONE ANOTHER.

never received from my sisters. Softness, openness, and a level of vulnerability is something I now look for in sister-friends. Fighting and conflicts in our neighborhood naturally made my sisters adopt an aggressive nature to protect themselves. Today I gravitate toward women who have free spirits and who've been able to or are working on peeling the layers of that aggression or trauma away. As Black women, we have not been afforded softness from others, and that negatively affects our intimacy with one another. We hold ourselves back from being in service of each other due to pride. A lot of women don't want to share their shit, not even with their friends, and that is a barrier to our connection. I wish the value of intimacy would translate to friendships among more Black women.

What I learned from my sisterhood at home is that you can be given the same type of love, the same opportunities, brought up with the same values, yet each of you can and will embark upon totally different paths and experiences. But the common thread woven between you never wavers: your values, your compassion, your commitment to see each other through your best and worst times. It's a union without obligations like that of a parent, or a commitment bound by the legalities and possessive conditions of marriage. It is purely free and should always be a place of solace.

I am better when I have a solid group of women with whom I can be vulnerable. Through mutual mentorships that reap rewards in other parts of my life—love, family, and career—and by sharing all the ways in which we've gotten things wrong, we can learn from one another. A safe space of reciprocity where we can exchange our talents and resources is how a village forms. Sisterhood that affirms what you know about yourself in moments of doubt is invaluable, and having that safe space where I can fully trust and be seen affirms me. It gives me the confidence and security I need to enter spaces I'm unfamiliar with because I know I have my safe haven of sisters to return home to. Being a sister is my most fulfilling and greatest role in life. It's what I know how to do best. It's innate, and it's groomed me through nurturing, from my sisters to my kindred spirits.

Human Nature

Having peace with the art of our messiness is more centering than anxiousness codependent on perfection. To understand this, I had to undo conditioning that compartmentalized vulnerability from strength. That conditioning will have us believe we can be in more control if we clench our fists around our insecurities. But needing space for vulnerability is human nature. When the world outside ourselves thrusts us into imbalance, accepting being a work in progress through the ebb and flow is an acceptance of ourselves in full.

Cradled by the Sun

Chloe Dulce Louvouezo

Starting a family was deeply personal. I selfishly wanted to make up for not having one of my own and wanted to redefine what family felt like. It helped to fill the gaps of my own wholeness by being the curator of someone else's. Having a child also meant an opportunity to pour into my son a sense of identity and belonging in a world that could ground him more than it ever did me. I knew my son would know where he was from and have a community that encouraged excellence in how he loved, fought, and found resolve in this world.

Yet, starting a family was not planned, and the timing of the pregnancy put a burden on me to spend my pregnancy alone—away from my child's father and my friends as I'd just relocated for a new job. I spent months in uncertainty and solitude. The experience of pregnancy didn't feel complete without their presence, and my excitement soon faded. I couldn't bring myself to fully usher in this new chapter with joy, and because of that, the sinking into depression was almost immediate. The excitement that I hoped to have in this budding season was lost to the disappointment of timing, and I felt guilty for my lackluster energy.

After a draining pregnancy, birth was an opportunity to be thoughtful in how I wanted to guide this new beginning. I decided to have a natural home birth for the chance to design my own experience. I intentionally wanted to lean into the fear of unmedicated birth to test my intrepidity. Working in partnership with the pain was my way of connecting with the baby despite having not enjoyed the journey of pregnancy. It was a way to be present with my body and to center myself through discomfort— an exercise in channeling the mental clarity I needed to push through. Birth became a perfect metaphor for how I've tried to move through life ever since.

The day I gave birth to Myel, the contractions pierced through every inch of my body, but the release of them was meditative, allowing the pain to run through me without attaching

Starting a family was deeply personal.... It helped to fill the gaps of my own wholeness by being the curator of someone else's.

my restless emotions to the pain itself. Birth was a spiritual experience that adorned my human experience. It was a reminder that when I feel that I have no more to give, I always still do. Our wells are never dry. It exemplified the way my own strength can increase in me when challenged by fear and that my fighting spirit is just a breath away.

The intimate bedroom home birth that welcomed our son into the world left us just as peaceful as it left us exhausted. Shortly after he belted out his first cries and the midwives hugged us goodbye, the three of us sank into the bed for our first family nap. I woke hours later with a new person buried in my chest and, as I smelled his hair and counted his toes, I waited for the beautiful tears of joy to set in as a crowning of motherhood. But they didn't—and I felt peculiarly empty. This was day one of the fourth trimester. In those first

The paranoia of being judged made condolences feel like pity and a rush to a goodbye that I wasn't ready for.

three months after the baby was born I didn't feel as agile as I always had in adjusting to a new normal. As much thought and time as I had put into my study of the forty weeks leading up to this climactic moment of bringing my son into the world, there was very little I knew about what to expect upon his arrival. I'd read up on the tricks of breastfeeding and managing bodily fluids, but no readings or words of wisdom from friends or family warned me of the emotional imbalance that would occupy this season.

After the wave of congratulatory visits from family and friends, we were left to fend for ourselves in our new roles as parents. Cluelessness, anxiety, and sleep deprivation—coupled with raging hormones that were at war with my mind—made for a disruptive spectrum of insecurities. I was discouraged by what felt like a lack of maternal instincts, and I was impatient to get

it right. My postpartum depression made me feel unstable, selfish, and inadequate. And guilty. Guilty that the hormones fostered neediness that neither I nor my partner recognized. Guilty for not enjoying every moment of this precious time. I quickly felt like I was losing my sense of self. What I knew myself to be—dynamic, passionate, sensible—felt like it was no more. And though I had the blessing of a patient partner and loving family and friends, few people asked how I was doing or would have understood. I felt let down by the experience. Those months post-birth brought out the rawest and realest bits of myself in ways only that experience could. As the first of my close friends to have a baby, the fourth trimester was on its best days lonely, and on its worst days depressing. I wish more candor existed in the conversations between women about the fragility of those months post-birth. I wish someone had told me that the feelings were normal and expected.

For a while, I lost my vitality through sleepless nights and I lost my wanderlust spirit through caretaking routines. I lost desires for old interests that were displaced by new priorities. My individuality felt absent postpartum. Sometimes we lose our old selves to find our new selves. Motherhood is a journey of undoing who you were and becoming who you are now with a child. We cling to the parts of ourselves that illuminate the life and possibility of what we could have done and who we could have been—and we mourn them when our identity shifts into motherhood. Once my days blossomed into a life of infectious baby giggles, my son's joy became contagious. In that joy, I was able to find my equilibrium between my past and my future. It has been a process of releasing control and being open to allowing how I see myself in this role as a mother to take new form. The experience of motherhood is raising both my son and me together.

In the journey of his life, Myel has had an innate gift of connection. And in recognizing that, his father and I decided to have a second child as our love offering to him. Intimate moments with the flutters and kicks inside my belly offered a newfound connection I didn't experience in my first pregnancy. I felt more present with our second son, Mali. I envisioned my two boys in company with each other in future hardship and joy, and the anticipation of their bond welcomed this new season for all of us. But while motherhood had just started to feel in flow, my relationship was not, and I battled panic attacks from the patterns of upheaval at home. One Tuesday morning, at twenty-seven weeks' pregnant, the fragility of my spirit and body got the best of me. I lost our baby son Mali in a stillbirth.

In the days, weeks, and months that followed, there was an emptiness in my womb that no condolences could heal—not even from my partner, whom I had grown to resent and increasingly pushed away. So I grieved alone. There's something about silence in solitude that is excruciatingly loud. My breasts were full of milk, my body full of agony, and my head full of questions. *Why me, why now*, they screamed. The loss was too abrupt to realize what had happened until I had already spent days staring out the window, bedridden, and surrounded by tissues and tea and shame and anger. I felt betrayed by the experience and that we had betrayed Mali. His conception had been a promise to protect him and it felt like failure. My heart was fatigued, and my grief was love with nowhere to go. I've never known such a feeling of helplessness.

When I started to leave the house, I was reminded of my empty womb when people who hadn't heard the news congratulated me, or worried and wondered, looked but didn't speak. It made me feel like I owed an explanation for a loss I hadn't yet come to terms with myself. I felt robbed of the sacredness my own processing deserved every time I locked eyes with gazes that posed questions. The paranoia of being judged made condolences feel like pity and a rush to a goodbye that I wasn't ready for. So I retreated back inside. For an entire year I stayed isolated,

THE SUN IS
PART OF OUR
FAMILY NOW—AN
INTERPRETATION
OF LOSS THAT I
WOULD HAVE NEVER
COME TO KNOW
WITHOUT HIM.

too protective of the space I was preserving for my processing. I took a sabbatical from work and used that time to decondition myself from what I thought motherhood should look like.

A big part of my loss was rooted in what I had envisioned our family would be. In some ways, I felt that growing our family validated my role as a mother by offering my son a brother—an extension of togetherness I never had myself. It satisfied a sense of responsibility and belonging for me, and admitting that has helped me understand my intentions for motherhood and the layered loss.

The grief over Mali remains ever-present. Not one day has gone by since April 17, 2019, that I haven't risen with a thought of him, an assurance that he *is* real and *is* mine still in heart and body. Even the emptiness of my womb cannot tell me that I am not a mother of two sons. My grief lives in my love for Mali as it does through the love I learn from Myel. No more was the belly he would kiss every day with sweet whispers of *I love you, brother*. Myel became convinced, through our telling of Mali having gone to heaven in the sky, that his brother was in fact the sun itself. Every day still, Myel speaks to the sun and of the sun. He dialogues every day with his brother when he wakes at his window in the mornings and consults him as he goes about his days. It's his way of paying homage to the brother he had connected with in the womb. As I honor the reminders of Mali, the space Myel has carved out for his brother is more sweet than bitter. The sun is part of our family now—an interpretation of loss that I would have never come to know without him.

Myel reminds us to start and end all things with love as they were intended, and that loss is not the end of our story. The impermanence and fragility of life now puts perspective on how we live our days, how I mother, and how I center myself in times of ambiguity. The journey to and through motherhood asks me to be a pillar when in fact it has been that for me. The woman I have discovered in motherhood allows grief and love and my old and my new selves to coexist. I am making space for them to feel whole together.

Recollecting Me

Qimmah Saafir
Founder, HANNAH *Magazine*

I grew up surrounded by powerful women, the main one being my mother. And as the middle child of her nine, I've always been privy to the realities of pregnancy, childbirth, and postpartum experience. When it came time to have my baby girl, I decided to have a natural birth. In my living room, in a pool, with a midwife. I experienced what is called prodromal labor, which is when labor starts and stops. Intense labor off and on for almost a week. By the time the actual labor that brought her earth-side began, I was exhausted. It was the hardest work I have ever done, but I have no regrets. There was such beauty in having my daughter laid on my chest right after she was born, looking at me, wide-eyed, in full health. To be able to lie with her in my bed without strangers, without wires, without cords. It was a true blessing.

After birth, I had her father, my mother, and a family of friends there to support me when they could. I can't imagine what those early months would have been like without them. So many women around the world are forced to do it alone. So, I am in full gratitude. But even in having that love and support, I felt alone at times. After family and friend visits, everyone goes home. As mothers, we're charged with keeping the baby healthy, alive, and thriving, despite not having a blueprint or reference

point for just how to do that . . . all while being significantly sleep deprived, with little energy. There are so many developments in those early months. Unless you have books to reference or people to push you in the right direction, you will feel absolutely lost and discouraged, particularly if you don't feel maternal instincts naturally and immediately kick in.

I knew that the fourth trimester existed and that it wasn't something that was often discussed. It can feel very isolating, like something is wrong. We don't always have the tools or the language to pinpoint what it is. Sometimes it's diagnosed as postpartum depression, sometimes it's just trying to find yourself again after birth. And often, it's the simple realization that you're not going to be the same person you were beforehand. I don't think we're really warned about that. We know we're going to be mothers, but no one talked to me about motherhood replacing individuality. For ten months, you are serving the purpose of growing your baby internally and bringing them earth-side. That's your focus. That's your purpose. Your love, health, and energy are pouring into that. Once that baby is here, a new mother might sometimes lack a sense of purpose or even identity, which can extend well beyond childbirth. As mothers, we often ignore our own needs as we pour into our little ones. Returning back to Qimmah and

> The newest part of my motherhood journey is allowing for reinvention and reassessment of self. It feels like a rediscovery.

redefining Qimmah means paying attention to how I'm loving myself, how I'm honoring myself, or how I'm pouring into myself.

I have always been so hard on myself, across the board. With so many siblings in our home, I always felt like I had to be A-plus in order to get some extra recognition or focused attention from my parents. They gave all of us love. But, that's a lot of children! They always told me they never had to worry about me. Unfortunately, never having to worry about me also meant knowing they could place their focus elsewhere. As a parent, I "overstand" that. As a child, that reinforced a level of self-expectation. A need to overachieve. And that definitely followed me into adulthood. Self-love through action is something I am still learning. My parents made sure we had a home, but we weren't well-off by any means. So as a large family, our love language was sacrifice. And that also followed me into adulthood, especially in romantic partnerships. It didn't feel right, in my body, to not constantly be of service and pour into others, even when I was empty. I am now working on undoing that. Learning how to say no to people and not feel guilty, to take pleasure and not feel guilty, to prioritize myself and not feel guilty.

The newest part of my motherhood journey is allowing for reinvention and reassess-ment of self. It feels like a rediscovery. Womanhood never leaves, the feminine never leaves. It just takes a redefining in this new space. My daughter is four years old, and I still grapple with who I am when she's not around. By taking care of everyone else, I have very much leaned into what I see as my masculine energy. As a provider and caretaker, when you're always being depended on, you have to carve out spaces to be more fluid. As hard as we are on ourselves, sometimes we need to have conversations with ourselves as if we're one of our own good girlfriends. It allows for a moment to intentionally step out of your mind to look at all that you do, and all that you are, and give yourself forgiveness, grace, upliftment, and room for reinvention. And when I find myself feeling lost or alone or down or unable to see outside of the present moment, I create a room in my mind where I see myself at almost every age. There's something about returning to that vision of walking up to myself, greeting her, embracing her, and thanking her. Returning to myself means returning to that room, and having some time with all of me.

Unlearning Strength

Josefina H. Sanders

Artist, Author, and Art Therapy Advocate

As women of color, we have a lot of unlearning to do.

Growing up in a Dominican home, I was taught never to discuss anything outside of happiness and passion, particularly mental illness. At a young age, I was wired to believe that strength meant to face raw emotions only in private, if at all. Thus, it was always challenging for me to open up and share deep parts of myself.

I didn't realize that I struggled with depression and anxiety until I got married. It was about two weeks after our wedding, and we were amid several transitions into our new life together. My girlfriends wondered why I was feeling down in what should have been a joyous time of my life. It wasn't until then that I realized that I was facing unresolved mental health challenges that I never had the opportunity to work through.

While I believe that there is beauty and wisdom in being private, I've found my strength in sharing some of my deepest struggles, especially in our filtered and curated world. Now that I have the opportunity to redefine strength, it means giving myself permission to heal. I find my strength through vulnerability.

Today, I choose to unlearn what society deems as strong, and I choose to live intentionally. As I live with intention, I ease into coming home to myself.

First, I reward myself. I comfort, encourage, and celebrate myself for a job well done and how I'm moving through life day by day. I allow myself to rest without guilt. I make any given day feel like a Sunday morning—slow and indulgent, taking time to relish it. I'm reminded to see the beauty in each day not just for the things I do, but for how I take care of myself.

It's been a journey full of heart and soul work to come home to myself. Doing so was most challenging when I had a pregnancy loss. I wasn't as mindful or intentional with myself before the miscarriage, and it took me a while to learn how to be good to myself. Often, I didn't understand whether my body loved me or hated me for breaking me in such a way that it didn't allow life to live in my womb. But I had to get to a place where I recognized the loss, and as I tended my grief, I found the strength in my body. Though I felt like my body had failed me, at that moment, it was the only thing I depended on to keep going and keep healing.

During the same season as the pregnancy loss, I came face-to-face with my mental illness and allowed my husband to see all of me. It was hard, especially during the moments it felt more comfortable to keep vulnerability at arm's length.

Like many, my husband didn't know much about depression. In my learning and unlearning journey, I had to learn that his support was

in his admittance of not knowing *how* to support. The same was true when we miscarried. As a couple, we had to figure out how to communicate with each other. We had to learn how to respond instead of reacting and to check in on each other's emotional well-being.

Today, I allow myself the time to figure out what it is that I need from him. Discerning when I share, while also setting boundaries in how and what I share with him. Six years later, we're still learning as we go on this journey of infertility. Battling depression and anxiety is even more challenging for me because there's still a part of me that feels uncomfortable opening up all the way. But allowing myself to share my insecurities with him has been insightful for him and healing for us.

When I realized that I was struggling with depression, I picked up a journal, and I taught myself calligraphy. I would write encouraging quotes to myself and how I felt in those moments. The paper was a place I could release every thought and struggle that entered my head. It became such a therapeutic and creative outlet and the beginning of how I started to affirm myself and speak words of life and truth through journaling. There was something so beautiful about spending so much time trying to learn how to form a letter. I was exploring my curiosity, and it became a meditative self-care practice. It was healing, it encouraged me to move with ease, and it was the very thing that kept my phone away. It allowed me to disconnect from my emotions and focus on the art. The more I learned about art therapy, the more I discovered my love for marrying it with mindful wellness. It's a way to cope with grief and hold ourselves accountable for expanding

curiosity about life. Creativity is alive in all of us, but many don't know what it looks like for them or have never explored it. Tapping into my creativity truly woke me up, and I can only hope others join in the awakening.

Beyond art therapy, my community is a massive piece of healing. There's such beauty in knowing that you're not the only one who has walked through what you've been through. There's also so much comfort in knowing who has shared experiences or who is triggered similarly. Having a community of women who really understand the same kind of pain and who have walked through that pain physically, emotionally, and mentally can be lifesaving. That community for me was formed through my opening up and sharing. Sharing out loud was like writing an apology letter to myself, allowing me to draw closer to myself and get out of my hole while having an anchor of support from other women. Being in a community amid healing reminds me that I am still alive and still loved.

There's such beauty in knowing that you're not the only one who has walked through what you've been through.

Intentional Motherhood, Exceptional Realness

Shay Jiles

Entrepreneur

I've shared openly about having obsessive compulsive disorder (OCD) over the years. My initial goal was to help others navigate it, but it was, honestly, for my own healing. Although I was clinically diagnosed with OCD in early college, I found that as I navigated adulthood, people were either dismissive about it or overly agreeable—saying things like, "I have OCD, too! I'm really organized!" or "I wash my hands a lot"—not fully understanding the magnitude of the habits and rituals tied to obsessive compulsive behaviors. It took a complete mental breakdown after being triggered by cutting my daughter's hair and having to cope with that perceived loss to really prompt me to speak on OCD and the various ways it manifests. I needed to speak out about what I was going through and what I was feeling. I was a strong woman on the outside, and everyone was giving me kudos—as a superwoman, supermom, and superwife. But I needed people to know that inside, I was obsessing over the smallest of things and that I didn't have control over the disorder. It was a relief for me to be able to share that side of myself with others, because it is such a big part of who I am.

Normalizing mental illness is therapeutic. You talk about it, you get it out, and you feel at peace with it. The more you share, the less it shocks others when you speak on it. My struggling with OCD and anxiety can now be approached with compassion and understanding from others. I've been able to build relationships with other women who share that they experience the same thing. It makes us all feel a little bit more normal in this world that is often dictated by superficiality.

Having OCD and anxiety, it's imperative for me to know my triggers, avoid them, and set boundaries. Boundaries have helped me filter how I spend my energy, as I am careful to not put myself in positions where I spiral into a black hole of being overwhelmed. When I started to know and listen to my triggers, I started exercising my power to say no. Sometimes that means not lending myself to the lives of those around me. It doesn't mean that I don't love them or care for them, but I have to, in that moment, choose myself and conserve my own energy. Sometimes it means passing up work opportunities. Sometimes it means not spreading my time thin or taking away from the moments I have with myself or my family to regroup. I need the space to release negative energy or anything that weighs me down. Whatever it is that I need to say no to in order to choose myself, I do, because I know that I can't truly show up for anyone if I'm not well. I have to pick and choose what I can do and be okay with whatever the consequences are around the things I cannot do. Those boundaries protect me and ultimately create a space that allows me to do more for others because I am prioritizing being good to myself first.

While sharing my struggles with OCD out loud is helpful, I've also come to learn that there is a clear difference between being transparent and being vulnerable. Being transparent, or simply sharing, is easier because I'm no longer emotionally bound to or I've completely healed from the disappointment, the trauma, or the overall experience. Vulnerability, on the other hand, is much more raw. It's deep-rooted, and my emotions are still invested. It's incredi-

bly hard to open myself up to the opinions and perspectives of others while sharing experiences that are so sacred to my heart or that I'm still learning to cope with, deal with, or learn from. My vulnerability comes in waves. I ask myself, "Do I really feel like this is something that God has for me to put out into the world?" Being vulnerable is much scarier than being transparent because I never know what the reaction's going to be. If someone says something the wrong way, it might be triggering. But when I am brave enough to be vulnerable, people are unexpectedly loving and welcoming. They are there to soak up what I have to say, and I'm there to soak up how therapeutic those exchanges can be.

As Black women, we're strong, we're fierce; we're an amazing body of women. But we're also in this "boss woman" culture where hustling is glorified and has become the standard for attaining success. Just because we can do it all, doesn't mean we have to or should. It's okay to say no. It's okay to not constantly hustle. It's okay to not do everything and to retire from constantly proving ourselves and feeling like we need to do more because the woman next to us is doing more. And it's okay to not constantly dive in or feel the need to keep up. That's when you start getting burned out and you start to hate what you do or what you thought you loved. It's time for us to be more gentle with ourselves and to trust that there are times when you are going to do more, and there are times where you have to sit back, relax, and simply process your vulnerabilities. I want all of us to spend more time in gratitude and being gentle with ourselves.

THERE IS A CLEAR DIFFERENCE BETWEEN BEING TRANSPARENT AND BEING VULNERABLE.

Pivoting to Reinvention

Danasia Fantastic
Creator, TheUrbanRealist

I worked in the hospitality industry from the time I was eighteen until 2013, when I started TheUrbanRealist. Working in hospitality made a lot of sense for me at the time because it was a great way to connect and meet people, and it was fast money being a bartender and a server. But I always knew I wanted to work for myself; I just didn't know what that looked like or how to go after it. I started TheUrbanRealist as a blog because I was passionate about writing. I didn't go full time with it until 2016, when one day, I went to the restaurant where I worked to check in for my shift and the building doors were locked. I didn't know why until the following day when I learned that the owner had avoided paying taxes for years and everything in the restaurant had been seized. That was a defining moment for me. I thought, if I was going to become an entrepreneur, this was the time. Losing that job freed me to go as hard as possible in building something for myself. It forced me to get creative. It forced me to get out there, and I knew that I had nothing to lose and everything to gain.

So often Black women put everyone else before ourselves. It's something that is expected. But continuing to put others' needs and expectations above your own desires, whatever is a priority to you, will weigh you down and rob you of the freedom to do what you really want to do. Pursuing dreams of our own liberate us from that. We need to realize our power and be okay with giving ourselves permission to take a leap of faith to go after our visions. Yes, we

might fail, but it's worth the risk if we feel we are being called to it. As an entrepreneur, there are ebbs and flows, something I knew very early on. I was groomed to understand that failure is part of the journey. My father has been an entrepreneur for most of my life. For years I thought, "This man is crazy," but in hindsight,

watching him work relentlessly allowed me to witness as a kid the power of not living in fear, and that's impacted me in how I move in life in such a positive way.

But the qualities that drive entrepreneurs are often the same ones that can work against us. Until the 2020 pandemic, I hadn't realized

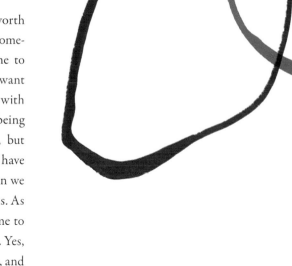

that for so long I had attached my self-worth to my productivity. I wanted to prove something to myself. The pandemic forced me to slow down and really reevaluate what I want out of my life and what I want to do next with entrepreneurship. I do find strength in being productive, which is all well and good, but I've also learned just how much we still have to come home to ourselves, especially when we don't have the outside world to stimulate us. As an entrepreneur, it's important to take time to discover what being still looks like for you. Yes, being productive, having faith, having grit, and being willing to be wrong and to take chances are all necessary. But being able to take a step back to get comfortable with who you are as a person without just letting what you do define you is also incredibly important—quarantine isolation helped me better understand that.

I'm a big believer in working in silence. Since my work depends on me being self-motivated, working from a place of thankfulness keeps me inspired, centered, and confident in my path. Nothing is ever guaranteed, but there's a huge "what if" or "what's next" right now for everyone challenged by the pandemic. No one knows what's ahead. I cope by trying to balance taking life one day at a time with also having a flexible action plan. Having some level of personal accountability in where I'm headed also motivates me when the rest of the world feels too ambiguous.

What I've learned most in my journey of entrepreneurship, and especially in this season as both the context of the world and my personal desires are changing, is that it's okay to let things go. It's okay to pivot. As I look back on the business I've built, I get excited about other things I want to do that require a deep dive. And in this continuous journey of learning and pivoting and reinventing, I've discovered that I don't know nearly as much as I always think I do. There's always room to grow. There's always room to learn. And in those lessons, I'm continuing to discover how to prioritize mental health. Just in 2020 alone, we're living through a pandemic and a revolution and, in a sense, we're in survival mode. For so long, everything I did was tied to work. Now, I'm realizing it's okay to sit and just be and not feel guilty about it. It's a privilege to be able to disconnect from the world. As we create new definitions of home for our communities and ourselves, home has become more than just a place to rest our heads at night. It's a place where we can feel safe enough to reinvent ourselves.

Go Forth and Be Dope

Julee Wilson
Beauty Director, Cosmopolitan *Magazine*

Showing up as our best selves every day is not an easy task. It is work. My joy is an act of survival and a conscious effort. I have to look at my blessings every day and not let the outside world kill my spirit. I set the intention of my energy early in my day before it slips through my fingers. Sometimes it's specific, but sometimes it's general, like believing and trusting in my magic. I have to say to myself: *You're golden. Don't let anything or anyone try to convince you otherwise.* By putting that messaging into the world, I've made it known to myself that believing in and manifesting those intentions are my mission. I check in with myself at the end of the day to determine whether I was true to my intentions. And if I wasn't, I don't beat myself up about it; but if I was, I give myself the credit.

Being intentional trickles into other areas of life. We live in a world of comparison. We hear a lot of, "You're not good enough. You're not pretty enough. You're not skinny enough. You don't have those shoes." That can get to you, even to the strongest people in the village. I'm proudly considered that strong friend in my village; however, I'm not as strong as people think I am. I try to pull back the curtain and show that not everything is perfect. Although I've had a successful career in my industry, I still live in a four-story walk-up in Harlem and

struggle financially. I still have to leave work to pick up my kid and balance motherhood and career. I still put on fake eyelashes to feel glamorous. I try to show the sometimes messy, imperfect side of life. So much of our world today is a farce, and it's important to dismantle false perceptions of perfection.

I put a lot of pressure on myself when it comes to my career. I give myself no other option but to win, to go hard, and to hustle, because I feel responsible for my family. I am of the mindset that I didn't come here to be mediocre. Too many people have sacrificed for me to be where I am, and now that I'm here, I try to be and do my best. That pressure is often accompanied by a lot of worry, which can feel like a sense of doom. We're taught that we shouldn't live in fear because it's the opposite of having faith. Yet it's not easy to reconcile the juxtaposition of living through the fragility of life while also trying to live in faith. To counteract the worry, I coach myself to sit in gratitude for the beautiful life that I am creating and the ways in which I'm already blessed. As I often worry about the future, making a conscious effort to be joyful centers me to stay present.

When you're being pulled in different directions and so much is required of you—from marriage to motherhood to career—pouring into yourself is a challenge. But as the years go

SO MUCH OF OUR WORLD TODAY IS A FARCE, AND IT'S IMPORTANT TO DISMANTLE FALSE PERCEPTIONS OF PERFECTION.

by, you learn to fall in love with yourself again and you think deeper into who you are and what your gems are. Today, I can sincerely say to myself, "I really like this chick, I dig her." I'm getting more comfortable with this post-pregnancy body, this skin, and the way my hair grows out of my head. I'm getting more comfortable with Julee, and I like showing that to the world.

We're not all perfect, but we're all we've got, so we have to work on being uniquely ourselves. When I walk into a room, I want to be very responsible for my energy and my vibration. I want people to see that I see them and to be an example of individuality—that I can be outspoken, silly, and quirky, and hopefully that inspires them to be more of themselves as well.

I can't imagine being on my deathbed when I'm old and gray and having regrets of trying to be someone I am not or not giving the world the best of me. I want to leave knowing I laid all my cards on the table. We all get into situations that don't necessarily feel like a fit, but I want to at least give myself the grace

to say, "If it doesn't fit, then work on trying to find something that does and don't persist in bullshit." Our time on earth is not guaranteed, and I don't want to ever know I wasted it on ill-fitting situations without leveraging my magic. To trust in our magic is to mute the voices around us that don't understand our worth. I say: manifest and leave the rest.

A Few Nights Under the Moonlight in Bahia

Doriana Diaz
Storyteller, Shapeshifter, and Sensitive Spirit

the first night/on the terrace at dusk overlooking the Salvador streets/we spoke of the women in white and voodoo/we spoke of home/and the places we mistakenly tried to build one in/we spoke of Cape Town where she grew up/tired and tender/we held hands tightly/made a promise that we would return to this land/and grow old here together/eventually evaporate into the sky/die holy in a place where/they would find us/one morning/tucked gently in our beds/still smiling.

under the moonlight a few days after/we all found our feet prancing right on the cusp of/where the ocean meets the sand/pulling our ankles out into the current/the water kissed every crevice of our skin/we floated out into the emptiness/skin shining like the dust from the sun/in the deepest part/we bounced with the weight of the waves/we watched the flesh on the shoreline/dance/giggle/drink/make love to the night.

one evening/in the middle of it all/there was a twitch/a sting and then a burning that crept its way through/every blood vessel/toes curling/at how my body needed to devour itself/scrape away the bits and pieces of decay I brought along with me/the land opened its womb/as I drifted closer to sleep/the nights rolled over themselves/into flashes/of uncut memories/leaking/specks of gold/onto my eyelids.

on our last night/all us black women let our thighs get angry/at the sound of bongo drums/our mouths dripping of slurs and love songs/our hips grinding as we cried sweet relief/we knew we had no more blood to lose/under the blowing banyan trees we laughed so hard our teeth/fell out at the roots/our bones fused together/we became a carnival/of shimmering skin/black in beauty/under the moonlight/the stars could have seen us smile.

With Intention

Chloe Dulce Louvouezo

There's this saying in French: *l'homme propose et Dieu dispose*, meaning man—or woman—proposes and God disposes. Our plans are irrelevant to Hers, and our destinies are not ours to control or pursue credit for. I've been reminded time and time again just how out of my control my life is and how much it is in Hers—a kind of surrendering that makes me weak in the knees but strong in the back. I don't have to project the future. I don't have to be consumed with knowing what's ahead. I can just be and be comforted and confident that how I show up in the world is all She needs to carry me through. My faith is in knowing that my presence on earth holds more weight than I have access to understand, so long as I loosen my reins while also living with intention. Being intentional for me means nothing can get past me without my conscious approval of its purpose in my life. It means getting our vertical alignment right, from God to our hearts to the direction of our feet before looking out to the world for answers. Sometimes we wait until it's convenient to do "the work" of vertically aligning. We wait until our hearts can no longer afford to, and we don't realize that autopilot is not serving us until we feel the effects of it intruding on our healing and our progress.

I have spent entire chapters of my life distracted. Distracted by the haunting of the past and worry about the future. Distracted by interpretations of circumstances that coddled insecurities and were barriers to my understanding how I could have been getting in my own way. Now, at moments of opportunity for distraction, I try to temperature check how my spirit reacts to discomfort and what it needs to feel safe. Without my being present with this active questioning, I am lost to any distraction that asks me to entertain it, and when I have done so, it has left me unrecognizable to myself. And that's a scary place to be. Today, the relationship I have with self-examination as a tool for living with intention makes me sit more upright in the moments of fight or flight. The practice of staying present has led to a pretty romantic relationship with life.

I began to scratch the surface of what it means to be intentional after a near-fatal car accident. I walked away from the crashed vehicle, its broken glass, and the upside-down frame without so much as a single bruise or cut, despite the airbag not having worked after the car flipped six times. The experience of being spared was jarring; logic would have deemed survival improbable. My faith in God ignited the next day, as if a formal introduction had greeted me at the very moment of vehicle impact. Being in proximity to death drove me to be more intentional about the woman I was to become while earth-side, which I didn't learn until years later I could only do by getting deeply acquainted with the girl I used to be. My life's work has been shapeshifting my inner child's blemished perception of herself. In the years that have followed, I have tried to find the discipline to be deliberate—but, admittedly, sometimes inconsistent—in filtering which narratives of myself do and don't belong in my spiritual ecosystem.

I'm still working through how to break away from limiting notions about myself and intentionally cultivate new definitions of who I am. No longer allowing emptiness to make decisions on my behalf and putting to rest old dreams that were conceived from a place of deficit have been two of my greatest shifts and gifts. Moving from the death of old ways to the birth of new ones is energizing. It is never too late to form new images of ourselves. It makes reinvention possible when we awaken an energy in us that we never realized had been in slumber.

But we're only capable of being intentional from where our perspective currently sits. It takes some living to inform the questions we ask ourselves, and it takes time to evolve how we want to show up in the world. I like the idea of continuously revisiting how we do both. And when the answers still aren't clear and there is still more exploring to be done, that, too, is okay. Not having answers doesn't invalidate the beauty and necessity of our stories. They will be written as the journey continues.

IT IS NEVER TOO LATE TO FORM NEW IMAGES OF OURSELVES.

ACKNOWLEDGMENTS

This book wouldn't be what it is without the contributors who saw the power of storytelling as a tool for healing and growth and who offered their own stories as examples of honest truth telling. My respect for you, your work, and your journeys goes further than any of these pages, and I am awed at your individual abilities to bring your experiences and your gifts to life in the ways you do. Thank you for sharing your voices, your beautiful voices, so that other Black women and all women can feel safer and more embraced in doing the same in their own healing. I am forever grateful to each of you for trusting me with this vision and its process. I am humbled that you saw purpose in this project.

Thank you to the listeners and guests of the *Life, I Swear* podcast for being so open to explore intimate conversations with me as I tried something new and stretched my own voice. Thank you for helping me make this storytelling work personally and communally restorative. In dialogue and in community, we are drawing connections between trials and triumph. We are mending our traumas through revolutionary thinking around what it means for Black women to survive, thrive, and discover ourselves.

Thank you to my mother, Agnya, Balkissa, Christy, for always allowing me to process my journey in my own time, on my own terms. The creativity and the exposure to the world that you showed me have shaped my worldview in ways that only you understand. Thank you for trusting my pace of life and for supporting Myel and me in every single season, the dark and the light. You have given me the freedom to fall and always try again.

Thank you to my auntie, kindred friend, and mentor Judith Jackson for your unwavering faith in me. "If it is meant to be, then it will be so," you told me the first day we met in your office at Services for the Underserved. God spoke to me that day through you, and I cherish you so. You have taught me self-respect and self-trust. I love you in ways I will never be able to articulate for how you have held my hand silently but tightly all these years.

To the women who are my chosen family, my true-blue friends. Elaine, you have shown me that love in its entirety, deeper and fuller than I had ever known, is possible and required. Thank you for being so invested in my prayers and for imagining the possibilities of this book beyond what I ever could. You have been my book doula through your blessing and support. Brooke, this life is our *Beaches*. Our sisterhood protects, trusts, validates, and perseveres. You have been my spiritual partner since the conception of *Life, I Swear* on Adam Clayton Powell Boulevard, and the rest has been history. Thank you for reminding me that our essence is all we need, and for letting us rest easy in all our dualities together. Offy, your constant love has helped me humanize myself. Thank you for being gentle when I've needed it most and for assuring all of me so that I could have the courage to translate it to paper. I love our unspoken understanding of this world that we will never outgrow. Adri, your voice of reason reminds me to stay centered. The home that lives in our friendship is a place I rely on to both hide from the world and refuel with more confidence. Kalkidan, sis, you gather me, each and every time. It is not at all by coincidence that our lives have been forever paired. For every ounce of heart that you've poured into my healing, I am stronger for it. Never have I known a love like yours. Natasha, my cheerleader in all things. I cherish the space we've created for celebration and belly laughs amid the world that would otherwise rob our joy. Crystal, you, my dear, are my definition of strength, family, and relentless pursuit of the truth. To be understood by you in this unconditional cousinhood has made pouring my own truth onto these pages feel like a responsibility to myself and to our constant examination of ourselves. This bowl of Life will always taste good sitting at the table with you. :)

To the friends who see me as a creative first. Thank you, Rob, for being a firm believer in *Life, I Swear* since it was a small blog with a lot of heart. Having you as an anchor fan and mentor through this work has been so much of the reason I've revisited the vision of this book since our days of email chains and creative minds, pun intended. :) To my loves L'Rai, Adiya, and Jasmine, thank you for coaching me to set boundaries in art and in life and to my day ones, Jo and Jessica, for believing that I could do this writing thing, or anything.

To Felice Laverne, who started off as my book coach and believed in this project enough to take me on as her first client as a literary agent. You held my hand through every draft and helped me see the parts of my story ready to be shared out loud and on paper. Without you knowing it, you helped grow my conviction that not telling these stories was not an option. There is not a world in which I could have embarked on this without you in this way, as aligned and as brave as you've helped me become as a writer. Thank you to my editor Soyolmaa Lkhagvadorj and the team at Harper Design for taking a chance on me and for believing in this book and appreciating my writing. Your trust in me as a first-time author has been affirming beyond measure.

Thank you to my people at the Bill & Melinda Gates Foundation. There is no other organization in the world that I would rather have spent my last six years with, through a journey of claiming my voice, through motherhood, and through some of my biggest personal growing pains and gains . I've been part of a community of colleagues and leaders at the foundation that recognize we are all people first. A special thank-you to my work wives Candi King and Melanie Brown for the well we share that never runs dry and for the kikis and reality checks that have kept me sane in this journey.

Thank you to Aileen Andrada, for holding me down at every stage of this book process. Your support has allowed me to simultaneously be a mother, writer, and entrepreneur with balance and ease.

WE ARE MENDING OUR TRAUMAS THROUGH REVOLUTIONARY THINKING AROUND WHAT IT MEANS FOR BLACK WOMEN TO SURVIVE, THRIVE, AND DISCOVER OURSELVES.

CONTRIBUTORS

Chloe Dulce Louvouezo

Chloe Dulce Louvouezo is a Congolese American writer and advocate for women. As a storyteller, she supports creativity and belonging of underrepresented women and seeks to deepen understanding of and within communities. Rooted in global citizenship, Chloe's fifteen-year career in communications has advanced diverse and inclusive storytelling at domestic and global organizations addressing education, poverty, and mental health, most recently at the Bill & Melinda Gates Foundation. She serves on the Washington, DC, Mayor's Commission for Women and is the executive producer and host of the popular *Life, I Swear* podcast, through which she explores nuances and insights around identity, mental wellness, and healing, told through the lens of women from the Black diaspora. Chloe is also a founding board member of HURU, which creates sacred spaces for rest experiences that foster emotional wellbeing and wholeness.

Eniafebiafe Isis Adewale

In one sentence, Eniafebiafe "Eniafe" Isis Adewale is a woman breaking into herself. Her leap into adulthood began at the age of sixteen when she journeyed three thousand miles from home to take advantage of a once-in-a-lifetime opportunity to study in New York City with the world-renowned Dance Theatre of Harlem. After graduating with a degree in sociology from Fordham University at Lincoln Center, Eniafe began her tenure at Rush Philanthropic Arts Foundation, where she established her grounding in the fields of event production and project management. Since her departure from the company in 2010, she's flexed some independent and entrepreneurial muscle and has continued to work with brands, both domestically and abroad, as event producer, project manager, and magic maker. A natural-born writer with a deep-rooted passion for narration and what she calls journey-telling, Eniafe is, as one colleague described, "an alchemist of emotion." Currently residing in Los Angeles, Eniafe is the chief experience officer of exi concepts and founder of ALL HER WORDS, a platform dedicated to honoring and amplifying the voices of a fuller spectrum of women.

Lauren Ash

Lauren Ash is a wellness visionary, yoga and meditation guide, engaging speaker and creative writer, and founder and executive director of the culture-shifting lifestyle brand synonymous with Black women's wellness: Black Girl in Om. Lauren has clarity about her purpose—she's here to expand the consciousness of Black women and women of color. Since founding Black Girl in Om in 2014, her vision has led to the creation of transformational experiences and of content that radically centers and authentically speaks to a historically and consistently marginalized global community. From executive producing and hosting the *Black Girl in Om* podcast—which has reached more than two million listeners within its four-season run—to touring the globe guiding meditations, yoga, and transformational conversations for thousands of Black women and women of color, Lauren has made contributions to the world that ultimately reflect what she once needed and didn't see.

Lauren has repeatedly been recognized as a trailblazer in the contemporary wellness movement. She has been affirmed for "fostering a community of healing" by the *New York Times*. She has been named "a master practitioner of #blackgirlmagic" and "a leading voice in the healthy-living world" by Well+Good. *Shape* has declared her "one of the most important voices in the wellness industry." And in 2019, she was one of *ESSENCE*'s Woke 100 and one of *Wanderlust*'s "35 under 35 in Wellness to Watch."

As a meditation and yoga teacher, Lauren centers compassionate presence, unconditional love, and intention. She is trained in Vedic Meditation with Ellie Burrows, and has received her two-hundred-hour certificates for Vinyasa Yoga with Koya Webb and Power Yoga with Ryan Loren. Lauren created a thirty-day Mindful Meditation Challenge for *Refinery 29*, shared her guidance for meditating with *O, The Oprah Magazine*, and produces ongoing audio meditations and digital meditation experiences for her global community.

Morgan Ashley

Morgan Ashley was born and raised in Oakland, California, but her nomadic spirit led her to Atlanta and into alignment with her current role as director of PR and operations for The Bohemian Brands. Destined to be anything but ordinary, Morgan is guided by her uncompromising, unapologetic pride in her Blackness and queerness as an entrepreneur and cultural purveyor. A connoisseur of culture, style, and cuisine, Morgan relied on these core tenets during her earliest days as an influencer and entrepreneur, launching the food discovery brand EatHereATL. It was also during this period of growth and discovery that she connected with business partner Vanessa Coore Vernon and conceived The Bohemian Brands, a joint venture created to rewrite the narrative behind the bohemian lifestyle and shed light on the intersectionality of social institutions such as race, sexuality, and gender. For Morgan, being Black is more than an identity; it is manna from heaven.

Esther Boykin

Esther Boykin is a relationship and marriage therapist and owner of Group Therapy Associates, a psychotherapy practice with multiple locations in the Washington, DC, metro area. Esther has a vision of making mental health widely accessible to all. Esther has extended her reach to other projects to further her mission for healthy relationships and accessible modern mental health. As CEO of Group Therapy Associates, Esther launched Therapy Is Not a Dirty Word, which hosts events and retreats and is also engaged in philanthropic efforts with Sidewalk Talk and Black Love Industry Professionals (BLIP). She also cohosts *With That Being Said*, a podcast with Erica Turner, and is featured regularly as an expert on shows like *Good Morning Washington* and the *Real Housewives of Potomac*. In between her myriad projects, Esther also provides professional consulting to mental health clinicians and weekend intensives for couples and families, focusing on dating and relationships, self-care, emotional intimacy, and various mental health topics.

Doriana Diaz

Doriana Diaz is a storyteller, shapeshifter, and sensitive spirit rooted in Philadelphia's soulful rhythms. She is the founder and curator of The Diaz Collections (@thediazcollections); an archival vessel channeling ancestral exploration of Black artistic wellness. Doriana is the self-published author of *Mami Calls Me Gabriella* and *Sun Phases*, both released in 2018. Her words have appeared in platforms such as; Nappy Head Club, Black Women Radicals, *GROWN* magazine, Saddie Baddies, SYLA Studio, Black Girl Magik, We Heal Too, The Kraal, and many more.

Alexandra Elle

Alexandra "Alex" Elle is an author and self-care facilitator living in the Washington, DC, metro area with her husband and children. Writing came into her life by way of therapy and the exploration of healing through journaling. Quarterly, Alex teaches workshops and retreats centered on assisting others in finding their voices through storytelling, poetry, and narrative writing rooted in truth without shame. Her mission is to build community and self-care practices through literature and language. She has published *In Courage* and *After the Rain* with Chronicle Books and has self-published a collection of journals, poetry, and essays.

Danasia Fantastic

Danasia previously lived in Philadelphia, Brooklyn, and Miami, prior to settling in Atlanta. Her interest in major-city culture inspired her to create something that encapsulated the energy she felt. Danasia has been featured in *Girlboss*, *ELLE* magazine, POPSUGAR, *USA Today*, and *Atlanta* magazine. She is also a former contributing writer for the Travel Channel, HGTV, and British Airways.

Lindsey Farrar

Lindsey Farrar is the cofounder and editor in chief of *CRWNMAG*, a premium print publication on a mission to be the most beautiful and honest representation of Black women in the history of print. Created to celebrate the whole Black woman, the publication uses natural hair as a lens through which to engage Black women in higher thought. Through beautiful content, thoughtful commentary, hair inspiration, and resources, *CRWNMAG* exists to edify and empower Black women across the globe.

Prior to releasing *CRWNMAG*'s first issue in August 2016, Lindsey worked for Interscope Records for six years and edited for various digital publications, before entering the start-up world. Witnessing the economic crash at the beginning of her career—after graduating from USC's Marshall School of Business—pushed Lindsey toward ownership, which started with her cofounding the online magazine *Made Woman*, another female-centered endeavor that helped women in the business world connect.

Lindsey is also currently the owner of Cadre, a creative consultancy and think tank.

Kalkidan Gebreyohannes

Kalkidan Gebreyohannes is an Ethiopian-born, Canadian-raised mother of three and entrepreneur based in Oakland, California. She is committed to celebrating and advancing her community through art, advocacy, and economic stability. Kalkidan is the owner of Blk Girls Green House, a plant and home goods shop launched in 2020. The space provides solace and reprieve and a sense of belonging for Black people and offers a space for humanity and joy to be celebrated and nurtured. Kalkidan is also co-owner of a women-owned Oakland boutique, Alyce on Grand, and a former designer for a high-end handbag and accessory line. She is a sought-after speaker, curator, and creative strategist in the Bay Area with a drive to inspire and support her community. She has been featured in *Forbes*, on KQED, and in *Bon Appétit*.

Brooke Hall

Brooke Hall, a Kentucky native, is passionate about integrating diversity in high-demand industries. She is an inclusion advocate with a mission to make career advancement opportunities accessible to creatives and digital talent. For more than ten years, Brooke has specialized in diversity recruitment and management of digital and creative projects. She is the founder of HueCap, a talent agency that connects businesses and federal agencies with Black talent and veterans who have high-demand skills in creative and tech spaces. She has also led operations, multicultural marketing, and production for companies and organizations such as the Thurgood Marshall College Fund, Amazon, Citigroup, Victoria's Secret, Greenhouse, and Ghost Note Agency.

Deun Ivory

Deun Ivory is a creative visionary, art director, multidisciplinary artist, photographer, and founder of the body: a home for love, a 501(c)(3) nonprofit shifting culture around how Black women heal from sexual trauma. She is a thought leader creating spaces and experiences that redefine what beauty and healing look like through creative wellness and visual storytelling. As one of the most important voices in the creative and wellness space, Deun has created some of the most profound work for brands such as Glossier, Apple, Girlfriend Collective, HBO, Nike, *CRWNMAG*, and many more. Her authenticity and commitment to amplifying the voices of Black women have empowered a generation of Black and brown communities to reclaim their beauty, their power, and their narratives.

Shay Jiles

Shay Jiles is a wife, mother of two, photographer, and creative residing in Texas, with a love for authentic communication and social interactions. She has a passion for honest parenting, encouraging self-love, and navigating mental health issues. Having OCD and anxiety herself, Shay aspires to normalize the conversations about mental health in the Black community and address the stigma surrounding it. She loves inspiring mothers to be intentional with how they pour into their children, encouraging them to be gentle with themselves, and reminding them of the power of setting boundaries. Her hope is to continue to give women and mothers a voice as well as a space for introspective and thought-provoking conversations to take place. Shay is a God-fearing woman, a truth teller, and has become known for her knack of delivering meaningful words, often accompanied by a side of humor.

Orixa Jones

Orixa Jones is a Los Angeles native and the founder of Bad Girl, Good Human, a platform to celebrate the multidimensional woman. Her work centers on visual artistry, expression, and the freedom for women to exist as themselves.

Nneka Julia

Nneka Julia is a writer, photographer, and podcast host based in Detroit, Michigan. As the daughter of immigrants hailing from Cambodia and Nigeria, her work is invariably tied to travel, culture, and the human experience. She married her passion for storytelling with several years of photographic training to produce product promotions, brand activations, and documentary projects for an array of global brands, ranging from the Four Seasons Hotels and Resorts to Starbucks Corporation. Her podcast, *Passing Through*, was ranked among the top one hundred podcasts in Apple's Society & Culture category in the US, streamed in over twenty countries, and sold out a two-hundred-person live show in NYC. She is currently working on writing her first book.

Lili Lopez

Senegalese visual expressionist Lili Lopez studied applied arts, photography, and business before working as a marketing director in media and entertainment in Paris. After she relocated to New York, her multimedia art practice gradually became her full-time occupation, and she now works across documentary films, watercolor pen on paper, and design. Lili's choice to embrace her natural creative ability is still very recent, but she has built quite the reputation for her geometrical, minimal, and African-inspired aesthetic. She has been commissioned by a wide range of clients as a creative strategist and/or illustrator. She also started the ongoing *UNDONE* series as a personal project that celebrates the importance of self-discovery and explores the concepts of creativity and identity. The debut series of *UNDONE* won the award for Best Web Series at the Bushwick Film Festival in 2016.

Meryanne Loum-Martin

International tastemaker Meryanne Loum-Martin is the designer and owner of the award-winning boutique hotel Jnane Tamsna in Marrakesh's Palmeraie district. She was born in Abidjan to a West Indian mother and a Senegalese father, and spent her adolescence and professional life in Paris. An heir to four generations of lawyers, Meryanne won the Prix des Secrétaires de la Conférence award as a lawyer before committing her life to design, hospitality, and architecture. Lauded in publications such as *Town & Country* and *Architectural Digest*, she has designed porcelain dinnerware and an outdoor furniture collection for Meissen. Her book *Inside Marrakesh: Enchanting Homes and Gardens* was published in September 2020.

Offeibea Obubah

Offeibea Obubah is a Ghanaian American writer and world traveler who believes in manifesting dreams and cherishing differences. She is a global health expert who has dedicated her career to problem-solving via innovative solutions to some of the world's biggest health disparities, such as maternal and newborn health, immunization, and access to medicines. She is a strategic technical officer in an international organization, where she works closely with over 190 countries in developing their national health agendas. Originally from Tema, Ghana, Offeibea has spent years living and working in the United States, United Kingdom, India, Ghana, Senegal, Tanzania, and Australia. She resides in Geneva, Switzerland.

Adriana Parrish

Adriana Parrish is an medium/intuitive healer who lives in Oakland, California, with her husband and daughter. She has embarked upon a journey of personal self-exploration through her own awakening and is on a mission to guide others on their healing journey. Adriana offers individualized and group intuitive healing sessions, mediumship readings, breathwork, and Reiki. She is in awe of the many healing modalities and always on a path for spiritual growth and enrichment. Her work as a channel or "conduit" of messages is a way to guide in connecting with one's higher self and bring healing. With a background in education and leadership development, she also specializes in spiritual wellness retreats and coaching to communities and corporate teams, with a particular focus on empowering diverse women through their healing practice.

Qimmah Saafir

Bronx-native Qimmah Saafir received her Bachelor of Arts degree from Spelman College in Atlanta before returning to New York to serve in a range of editorial capacities within the magazine industry for more than a decade. While working with publications such as *InStyle*, *Marie Claire*, *Lucky*, and *W*, Qimmah witnessed and attempted to remedy an outstanding lack of diversity and inclusion in the offices and pages of many mainstream magazines. In response, Saafir concluded her freelance career and created and self-published *HANNAH*, an independent journal that celebrates and provides safe spaces for Black women. Each edition of *HANNAH* showcases the diversity and influence of Black women across numerous fields. Recognized for her ability to authentically tap into a niche audience, Qimmah has since assisted individuals, brands, and companies including BAM, Walker & Company, and IDEO.org with troubleshooting, targeted marketing, and content creation. The multihyphenate intends to continue carving out inclusive spaces across all media. Her upcoming work includes several on-screen projects. She also cofounded Ps&Qs, a publishing company created to encourage diversity in children's literature, and penned the company's first book, titled *Charlie & His Imaginary Friend*.

Josefina H. Sanders

Josefina H. Sanders is an artist, author, mental health advocate, and art therapy student living and working in Tampa, Florida. As someone who has struggled with depression and anxiety, Josefina uses powerful words and meaningful visuals to raise awareness of mental health and wellness. She has authored her first book, *The Mourning Sister*, a collection of poems and prose that explores the journey of grief and joy. Josefina also leads creative workshops and coaching for people looking to explore art therapy as a means to mental health recovery and personal healing.

Dydine Umunyana

Dydine Umunyana is a cohost of *Umuco Podcast* and author of the book *Embracing Survival*, a memoir that tells the story of the 1994 Rwandan genocide against the Tutsis at the hands of Hutu perpetrators through the eyes of her four-year-old self when the horrific massacre occurred.

In 2013, Dydine was appointed as a youth peace ambassador for the Aegis Trust, an organization dedicated to the prevention of genocide and mass atrocities worldwide. Subsequently, in 2015, she became a Global Mentor for Peace at Serve to Unite, an organization that cultivates peace through creative service learning and global engagement. Now she is the cofounder of Umuco Love, an organization that focuses its efforts on fostering cultural understanding among young people from all backgrounds using storytelling as a tool. Dydine is committed to establishing a dialogue among people for understanding their shared histories and cultural differences. Through writing and public lectures, her goal is to pierce the wall of division that still pervades much of our society.

Elaine Welteroth

Elaine Welteroth is a *New York Times*–bestselling author, award-winning journalist, and judge on the show *Project Runway*. She is known for her groundbreaking work at the helm of *Teen Vogue*, where in 2017 she was appointed the youngest editor in chief at a Condé Nast publication. She is a leading expert and advocate for the next generation of change makers. She was recently appointed cultural ambassador for Michelle Obama's When We All Vote initiative. She has written for the hit show *Grown-ish* and has appeared on camera for a range of media outlets, including ABC News and Netflix. Her debut book, *More Than Enough,* became an instant bestseller in 2019 and received an NAACP award in 2020. In 2021, she joined CBS's *The Talk* as a cohost.

Gabrielle Williams

Born in Atlanta and raised in Maryland and Washington, DC, Gabrielle is a multidisciplinary teacher and holistic healer. Among her greatest influences have been womanist-centered education at Spelman College; her talented multigenerational family full of doctors, artists, and teachers; and her training in shamanic and ancestral healing in Brazil.

She began her teaching career in Spain, educating elementary students in a Catholic school. From there, she returned to the US for a stint in the US Department of State at the office of Secretary Hillary Clinton. She returned thereafter to her calling as a teacher in Brazil. In Salvador, Brazil, Gabrielle further blossomed not only into an effective and loving educator, but also into a competent cofounder of a flourishing English-language consulting business, As Gringas. In addition, Gabrielle's time in Brazil was marked by her integration into local holistic and shamanic healing communities. There, she was chosen to apprentice under senior community healers and was charged with assisting them in illuminating the wisdom of various spiritual traditions and ancestors for the benefit of all who seek inner peace and self-healing. Over the course of her ongoing apprenticeship, she became adept in a number of healing modalities: Reiki, sound healing, and plant medicine.

Gabrielle is the proud mother of a three-year-old son, Milo. Her work, both in the education and holistic wellness fields, is dedicated to paving the way for a more just, peaceful, and enlightened world for her son and other youth to flourish in.

Julee Wilson

Julee Wilson is beauty director at *Cosmopolitan*. In her role, Wilson leads the brand's robust beauty coverage across all platforms, spearheading coverage in print, digital, and social media and creating new ways of reaching readers.

Previously, Julee was global beauty director at *Essence* and also served as fashion & beauty director there for three years. In addition, she has held editorial positions at *Huffington Post* and *Real Simple*. Throughout her career, Julee has appeared on CNN, *The TODAY Show*, CBS's *The Early Show*, and ABC's *Nightline*, and *Access Hollywood*. Her byline has also has appeared in *InStyle*, *Condé Nast Traveler*, *Vibe*, *Business of Fashion*, and *International Journal of Fashion Studies*.

Julee is an alum of the University of Richmond and Stanford University's Professional Publishing Course. She sits on the advisory board of Harlem's Fashion Row and is a member of Alpha Kappa Alpha Sorority, Inc. Julee resides in Harlem with her brilliant husband, two children, and massive shoe collection.

PHOTOGRAPHY CREDITS

Eniafebiafe Isis Adewale: Photographs by Ser Baffo

Lauren Ash: Photographs by Taylor S. Hunter

Morgan Ashley: Photographs by Kelley Raye

Ester Boykin: Photographs by MF.Jonez from Marsh Kove Media

Doriana Diaz: Photographs by Doriana Diaz

Alexandra Elle: Photograph by Alexandra Elle

Danasia Fantastic: Photographs by Savanna Sturkie from Savanna Sturkie Photo

Lindsey Farrar: Photographs by Nkrumah Farrar, courtesy of CRWNMAG

Kalkidan Gebreyohannes: Photographs by Samantha Tyler

Brooke Hall: Photographs by Erik Branch

Deun Ivory: Photographs by Deun Ivory

Shay Jiles: Photographs by Tosha Chaney

Orixa Jones: Photographs by Orixa Jones

Nneka Julia: Photographs by Nneka Julia

Lili Lopez: Photographs by Kivvi Rachelle

Meryanne Loum-Martin: Photograph by Alena Torgonskaya

Chloe Dulce Louvouezo: Photographs by MF.Jonez from Marsh Kove Media: 20–21, 22, 46–47, 48–49, 74–75, 97, 100, 172-173; photographs by Storytellez: 11, 76–77, 120, 123, 145, 149; photographs courtesy of Chloe Dulce Louvouezo: 50–51

Offeibea Obubah: Photographs by Muse Mohammed

Adriana Parrish: Photographs by Samantha Tyler

Qimmah Saafir: Photographs by Joe Chea

Josefina H. Sanders: Photographs by Josefina H. Sanders

Dydine Umunyana: Photograph by Dan McMahon

Elaine Welteroth: Photograph by Marlowe Granados

Gabrielle Williams: Photographs by Jonathan van de Knaap

Julee Wilson: Photographs by Joe Chea

© Creative Fabrica/Bron Alexander: 35 (bottom), 82 (top), 92, 157 (bottom), 174 (bottom)

© Creative Market/Lana Elanor: 7 (bottom), 19 (top), 26, 114 (bottom), 165

© Getty Images/boggy22: 142–143

© Shutterstock/Apostrophe: 148, 175

© Shutterstock/BGStock72: 94–95, 118–119

© Shutterstock/HSk Art: 17, 115, 140

© Shutterstock/Khazanova: 18 (bottom left), 73 (bottom right), 117 (top right)

© Shutterstock/KsushaFineArt: 14, 127, 179

© Shutterstock/StreetVJ: 27

© Shutterstock/VerisStudio: 5, 7 (top), 13, 18–19 (background), 25, 35 (top), 40, 52, 53, 57 (bottom), 60, 61, 64, 71, 72–73 (background), 78, 82 (bottom), 85, 89, 93, 99, 101, 105, 110, 116–117 (background), 122, 126, 130, 135, 138, 141, 147, 153, 157 (top), 169 (top, bottom left), 174 (top)

© Shutterstock/White snow: 31, 39, 106, 161, 168